The Complete Fan's Comp

The Complete Fan's Companion to EURO 2024

An Unofficial Guide to the Groups, Schedule, Venues, and Other Details

Paul Refuge

The Complete Fan's Companion to EURO 2024

Copyright © 2024 JayPaul Publishers

All rights reserved. No part of this publication may be reproduced, distributed, or transmitted in any form or by any means, including photocopying, recording, or other electronic or mechanical methods, without the prior written permission of the publisher, except in the case of brief quotations embodied in critical reviews and certain other noncommercial uses permitted by copyright law. For permission requests, please contact the publisher.

ISBN: 9798326033154

The Complete Fan's Companion to EURO 2024

Dedication

To the beautiful game of football and its passionate fans across Europe.

The Complete Fan's Companion to EURO 2024

Acknowledgement

I would like to express my sincere gratitude to my readers for their support and interest in this EURO 2024 unofficial guide. Your enthusiasm for the tournament inspired me to create this book.

A special thanks to my publisher for believing in this project and providing me with the opportunity to share my insights and knowledge about one of the biggest football events in the world. Your guidance and efforts have been invaluable.

The Complete Fan's Companion to EURO 2024

Table of Contents

Dedication   3

Acknowledgement   4

Table of Contents   5

Introduction   8

Chapter 1: Overview of Euro 2024 in Germany   10

Chapter 2: Host Cities and Venues   14

    2.1 Berlin   15

    2.1.1 Olympiastadion   25

    2.2 Dortmund   34

    2.2.1 Signal Iduna Park   40

    2.3 Düsseldorf   48

    2.3.1 Düsseldorf Arena/Merkur Spiel-Arena   54

    2.4 Frankfurt   60

    2.4.1 Deutsche Bank Park   70

    2.5 Gelsenkirchen   75

The Complete Fan's Companion to EURO 2024

2.5.1 Veltins-Arena	79
2.6 Hamburg	88
2.6.1 Volksparkstadion	94
2.7 Cologne	99
2.7.1 RheinEnergieStadion	109
2.8 Leipzig	118
2.7.1 Red Bull Arena	128
2.8 Munich	133
2.8.1 Allianz Arena	138
2.9 Stuttgart	145
2.9.1 Stuttgart Arena Stadium	152

Chapter 3: History of the UEFA European Championship — **159**

3.1 Records and Statistics — 176

Chapter 4: Groups and Teams — **195**

Chapter 5: Group Stage Draw Analysis — **199**

5.1 Group B Analysis — 211

5.2 Group C Analysis	217
5.3 Group D Analysis	225
5.4 Group E Analysis	236
5.5 Group F Analysis	244
Chapter 6: Germany Likely Team Profile	**255**
Chapter 7: Tournament Schedule	**257**
7.1 Knockout Stage Overview	261
Chapter 8: Germany Hosting History at EURO	**265**
Chapter 9: German Legends	**285**
Chapter 10: German Football Culture	**346**
Chapter 11: Future Host Nations	**354**
Chapter 12: Euro 2024 Match Officials	**364**
Chapter 13: The Euro 2024 Match Symbols	**366**
Conclusion	**368**
REVIEW	**371**

The Complete Fan's Companion to EURO 2024

Introduction

The UEFA European Championship is one of the biggest football tournaments in the world. Every four years, the best national teams from across Europe compete to be crowned champions.

In 2024, the Euro championship will take place in Germany from June 14th to July 14th. This will be the second time Germany has hosted this major tournament, after previously hosting in 1988 when it was West Germany.

A total of 10 stadiums in 10 different German cities will host the Euro 2024 matches. The host cities are Berlin, Dortmund, Düsseldorf, Frankfurt, Gelsenkirchen, Hamburg, Cologne, Leipzig, Munich and Stuttgart.

The Complete Fan's Companion to EURO 2024

The best 24 national teams will qualify to play in the tournament. They will be split into six groups of four teams each for the group stage. The top two teams from each group will advance to the knockout rounds.

This book is an unofficial guide to help fans prepare for and follow the Euro 2024 action in Germany. Inside you'll find details on the host cities, stadiums, groups, schedule and more. Whether you're traveling to Germany or watching from home, this guide will enhance your Euro 2024 experience.

Get ready for an incredible festival of football across Germany! Euro 2024 is shaping up to be an unforgettable event.

The Complete Fan's Companion to EURO 2024

Chapter 1: Overview of Euro 2024 in Germany

The 2024 UEFA European Football Championship, commonly called Euro 2024, is the 17th edition of this major men's national team tournament for European countries organized by UEFA. Germany is hosting the event from June 14 to July 14, 2024. The Euro 2024 winner will play against the 2024 Copa América champion in a special match.

A total of 24 teams will participate at Euro 2024, with the country of Georgia making their debut appearance at the European Championship finals. This marks the third time Germany has staged European Championship matches, but it is the first time a reunified Germany is the sole host nation.

Specifically:

It was hosted by West Germany in 1988.
Four matches of the multi-national Euro 2020 tournament were played in Munich, Germany.
And now in 2024, a reunified Germany will serve as the sole host nation for the entire European Championship finals for the first time.

The defending Euro champions are Italy, who defeated England on penalties in the final of the postponed Euro 2020 tournament.

Germany was chosen as the Euro 2024 host by the UEFA Executive Committee in September

The Complete Fan's Companion to EURO 2024

2018, receiving 12 votes compared to 4 for the other bidder Turkey.

Ten stadiums in 10 different German cities will host the Euro 2024 matches: Berlin, Munich, Dortmund, Stuttgart, Gelsenkirchen, Frankfurt, Hamburg, Düsseldorf, Cologne and Leipzig. Nine of these venues were also used for the 2006 FIFA World Cup in Germany.

The 24 qualified teams will be based at designated team camps located around Germany during the tournament, using these as their home bases for accommodation and training between matches.

In qualifying, Portugal, France, England, Belgium, Hungary and Romania managed to reach Euro 2024 without losing a single game. Georgia secured their first ever qualification for a major tournament by beating Greece in the playoffs.

Notable teams that failed to qualify include Sweden, Russia (who were banned from participating due to the invasion of Ukraine), and Wales.

The final tournament draw in December 2023 set the six groups of four teams each for the Euro 2024 group stage.

The Complete Fan's Companion to EURO 2024

Chapter 2: Host Cities and Venues

UEFA EURO 2024 will happen in Germany. Ten big stadiums in different cities will host the games.

The cities are Berlin, Cologne, Dortmund, Düsseldorf, Frankfurt, Gelsenkirchen, Hamburg, Leipzig, Munich, and Stuttgart.

The stadiums include famous ones like the Olympiastadion in Berlin, Signal Iduna Park in Dortmund, and Allianz Arena in Munich.

All these stadiums are large and modern. They can hold many thousands of fans. The stadiums will provide great places for the EURO 2024 football matches.

2.1 Berlin

Berlin, the capital of Germany, is a city that has witnessed a tumultuous history, yet it stands tall today as a vibrant metropolis that blends modernity with its rich cultural heritage. With a population of over 3.8 million, it is the most populous city in the European Union and the second-largest metropolitan region in Germany, after the Rhine-Ruhr region.

This city is a true embodiment of contrasts, where the remnants of its turbulent past coexist harmoniously with its modern, cosmopolitan character. From the iconic Brandenburg Gate, a symbol of unity and freedom, to the graffiti-covered remnants of the Berlin Wall, a chilling reminder of the city's divisive history. The city of Berlin presents a diverse blend of activities and attractions.

Major Attractions and Landmarks:

1. **Brandenburg Gate**: This neoclassical monument, built in the late 18th century, stands as a proof of Berlin's strength. Once a symbol of division during the Cold War, it now celebrates the city's unity and serves as a popular gathering place for locals and tourists alike.

2. **Museum Island**: A UNESCO World Heritage Site, Museum Island is home to five world-renowned museums, including the Pergamon Museum, known for its ancient Greek

and Babylonian artifacts, and the Neues Museum, which houses the iconic bust of Queen Nefertiti.

3. **Berlin Wall Memorial**: While only a small portion of the Berlin Wall remains, the East Side Gallery is a powerful reminder of the city's divided past. This open-air gallery stretches for nearly a mile and features over 100 murals painted by artists from around the world.

4. **Reichstag Building**: Once the home of the German Parliament, the Reichstag Building was heavily damaged during World War II. After reunification, it was beautifully restored, complete with a stunning glass dome that offers panoramic views of the city.

5. **Charlottenburg Palace**: This stunning Prussian palace, with its exquisite gardens and elaborate

architecture, provides a glimpse into Berlin's royal past and serves as a popular destination for those seeking a taste of opulence.

Recommended Neighborhoods to Visit:

1. **Mitte**: Berlin's historic center, Mitte is a must-visit neighborhood for anyone seeking to immerse themselves in the city's cultural heritage. From the iconic Gendarmenmarkt square to the vibrant Hackesche Höfe courtyards, this area offers a unique blend of history and modern urban life.

2. **Kreuzberg**: Known for its alternative culture and vibrant street art scene, Kreuzberg is a haven for artists, musicians, and those seeking a more bohemian atmosphere. The neighborhood's diverse culinary offerings and lively nightlife

make it a popular destination for locals and visitors alike.

3. **Prenzlauer Berg**: Once a part of former East Berlin, Prenzlauer Berg has transformed into a trendy neighborhood with a thriving art scene, quirky cafés, and charming boutiques. Its tree-lined streets and beautifully restored Altbau buildings add to the area's undeniable charm.

Berlin is well-connected by a comprehensive transportation network, making it easy to navigate the city.

- **Airports**: Berlin is served by the Berlin Brandenburg Airport (BER), which replaced the former Tegel and Schönefeld airports. This modern airport facility is located just outside

Berlin's southeastern border and offers convenient access to the city center.

- **Rail**: Long-distance rail lines connect Berlin to major cities across Germany and beyond, while the regional rail system (S-Bahn) provides efficient transportation within the city and its surrounding areas.

- **Metro/Tram**: Berlin's extensive U-Bahn (underground) and tram systems are reliable and efficient, making it easy to explore different parts of the city without relying on personal vehicles.

Berlin has also hosted numerous significant sporting events throughout its history, including:

- **1936 Summer Olympics**: The city hosted the Summer Olympics at the iconic Olympiastadion, which also played host to the 2006 FIFA World Cup final.

- **2009 World Athletics Championships**: The Olympiastadion once again took center stage for this prestigious athletics event, showcasing the city's ability to host major international competitions.

- **2015 UEFA Champions League Final**: Berlin's reputation as a world-class sports destination was further solidified when it hosted the highly anticipated UEFA Champions League final at the iconic Olympiastadion.

- **2023 Special Olympics World Summer Games**: In a historic first, Germany hosted the Special

Olympics World Summer Games in Berlin, on 17 June 2023 – 25 June 2023, showcasing the city's commitment to inclusivity and celebrating the achievements of athletes with intellectual disabilities.

Berlin's Culinary Scene:

Berlin's culinary offerings are as diverse and eclectic as the city itself. From traditional German fare to international cuisines, the city's food scene caters to every taste and preference.

1. **Traditional German Cuisine**: No visit to Berlin is complete without savoring the city's iconic dishes, such as currywurst (a sausage smothered in a curried ketchup sauce), buletten (meat patties), and the beloved Berliner doughnut, known locally as pfannkuchen.

The Complete Fan's Companion to EURO 2024

2. **Multicultural Flavors**: Berlin's rich immigrant history has influenced its culinary landscape, with Turkish and Arab communities bringing their delectable dishes like lahmajoun (Turkish flatbread) and falafel to the city. The modern doner kebab sandwich, which originated in Berlin in the 1970s, has become a popular street food staple not only in the city but around the world.

3. **Innovative Gastronomy**: Berlin's food scene is not just about traditional fare; it's also a hub for innovative and experimental gastronomy. From pop-up street food markets to supper clubs and food festivals like Berlin Food Week, the city's culinary landscape is constantly evolving, embracing sustainable and locally sourced

ingredients while pushing the boundaries of flavor combinations.

4. **International Cuisines**: Berlin's cosmopolitan character is reflected in its different array of international restaurants. Whether you're craving Asian flavors like Chinese, Vietnamese, Thai, Indian, Korean, or Japanese, or seeking out Spanish tapas bars, Italian trattorias, or Greek tavernas, the city's dining scene has something to offer for every palate.

With its rich culinary heritage and a thriving gastronomic scene, Berlin is a true food lover's paradise. From indulging in traditional German delicacies to exploring the city's multicultural flavors and innovative dining experiences, Berlin's culinary promises a delightful and unforgettable journey for the senses.

Berlin is a city that defies simple descriptions. It is a place where history and modernity collide, where art and culture thrive, and where freedom is celebrated. Berlin promises an experience that will leave a lasting impression when you visit.

2.1.1 **Olympiastadion**

The Olympiastadion in Berlin, Germany, is a world-renowned sports venue that has witnessed numerous historical events and hosted prestigious international competitions. Originally constructed for the 1936 Summer Olympics, this stadium has undergone several renovations and remains an architectural marvel.

The Olympiastadion is situated in the Olympiapark Berlin, located in the Westend area of the Charlottenburg-Wilmersdorf district in Berlin, Germany. Its address is Olympischer Platz 3, 14053 Berlin.

After the most recent renovations in 2004, the Olympiastadion boasts an impressive permanent seating capacity of 74,475, making it the largest stadium in Germany for international football matches. Additionally, for certain high-profile events, the capacity can be temporarily expanded to accommodate up to 76,197 spectators by adding mobile grandstands over the Marathon Arch.

The Olympiastadion was initially constructed between 1934 and 1936 under the supervision of architects Werner March and Albert Speer, designed specifically for the 1936 Summer Olympics. It underwent its first major renovation in 1974 by architect Friedrich Wilhelm Krahe, followed by a comprehensive €242 million renovation project from 2000 to 2004 in preparation for the 2006 FIFA World Cup.

The Olympiastadion's unique design features a lower bowl recessed 12 meters (40 feet) below ground level, providing a distinctive and intimate atmosphere for spectators. The renovation in 2004 saw the addition of a striking translucent roof spanning 37,000 square meters (400,000 square feet), supported by 20 columns carrying 3,500 tons of steel. The roof's western portion remains open, revealing the historic Bell Tower to spectators.

The playing surface at the Olympiastadion is a natural grass field, measuring 105 meters by 68 meters (344 feet by 223 feet).

The Olympiastadion has played host to numerous significant sporting events throughout its illustrious history:

1936 Summer Olympics: The stadium hosted the opening ceremony and various athletic events, including track and field, football, handball, and equestrian competitions during the 1936 Olympics.

1974 FIFA World Cup: Three group stage matches were held at the Olympiastadion during the 1974 FIFA World Cup.

2006 FIFA World Cup: The stadium hosted six matches during the 2006 FIFA World Cup, including the highly anticipated final between Italy and France.

2011 FIFA Women's World Cup: Germany's opening match against Canada in the 2011 FIFA Women's World Cup was played at the Olympiastadion.

2015 UEFA Champions League Final: The prestigious 2015 UEFA Champions League Final between Juventus and Barcelona took place at the stadium, with Barcelona emerging victorious.

2023 Special Olympics World Summer Games: The Olympiastadion hosted the opening ceremony of the 2023 Special Olympics World Summer Games on June 17, 2023.

The Complete Fan's Companion to EURO 2024

UEFA Euro 2024: The stadium is scheduled to host six matches during the upcoming UEFA Euro 2024, including a round of 16 match, a quarter-final, and the tournament's final on July 14, 2024.

In addition to these major events, the Olympiastadion has been the home venue for the Bundesliga club Hertha BSC since 1963, hosting numerous domestic league matches and cup finals over the years.

The Olympiastadion in Berlin will host several crucial matches during the UEFA Euro 2024 football tournament.

On June 15th, at 6:00 PM, the Olympiastadion will witness an exciting Group B clash between two European football giants, Spain and Croatia. Both teams boast talented squads and have a good history in international competitions, making this match a highly anticipated encounter.

Six days later, on June 21st, at 6:00 PM, the stadium will host another Group D match, this time featuring Poland and Austria. These two neighboring countries will battle it out on the pitch, with both teams aiming to secure crucial points in their quest to advance to the knockout stages.

On June 25th, at 6:00 PM, the Olympiastadion will once again be the venue for a Group D match, as the Netherlands take on Austria. The Dutch team, known for their attractive playing style, will face a tough test against the Austrians in what promises to be an intriguing encounter.

As the tournament progresses, the Olympiastadion will host one of the round of 16 matches on June 29th, at 6:00 PM. The runners-up from Group A and Group B will clash in this knockout game, with the winner advancing to the quarter-finals.

The excitement will continue on July 6th, at 9:00 PM, when the Olympiastadion hosts one of the highly anticipated quarter-final matches. The winners of two previous rounds of 16 matches will compete for a spot in the semi-finals, bringing the tournament closer to its climax.

Finally, on July 14th, at 9:00 PM, the Olympiastadion will have the honor of hosting the UEFA Euro 2024 final. This is the pinnacle of the tournament, where the two remaining teams will battle it out for the coveted European Championship trophy. Football fans around the world will be glued to their screens, witnessing the crowning of a new continental champion at this historic venue.

With its lovely history, impressive capacity, and state-of-the-art facilities, the Olympiastadion in Berlin is a fitting stage for these crucial matches during the UEFA Euro 2024. Football enthusiasts can look forward to witnessing some of the best teams and players in Europe compete at this iconic stadium, creating unforgettable moments and memories.

The Olympiastadion is a true architectural masterpiece and a strong proof of Germany's well-grounded sporting history. Its ability to adapt and evolve through renovations has ensured that it remains a world-class venue, capable of hosting the most prestigious international sporting events. With its unique design, impressive capacity, and storied past, the Olympiastadion continues to captivate spectators and athletes alike, cementing its place as one of the most iconic and significant stadiums in the world.

2.2 **Dortmund**

Dortmund is the third biggest city in the state of North Rhine-Westphalia in Germany. It has over 600,000 residents, making it the largest city in the Ruhr region and the biggest city in the Westphalia area. Dortmund sits on the Emscher and Ruhr rivers which flow into the Rhine River. It is located in the Rhine-Ruhr Metropolitan Region, the second biggest metropolitan area by economic output in the whole European Union. Dortmund is considered the administrative, business, and cultural hub of the eastern part of the Ruhr region.

Dortmund is a major road transport crossroads in Germany with several major highways passing through or around the city like the A1, A2, A45 and the Ruhrschnellweg expressway. While efficient, the Ruhrschnellweg is actually very congested and often called "the Ruhr area's longest parking lot."

Cycling is promoted in Dortmund with an extensive network of bike paths that grew popular starting in the 1980s. The city even has a special fast bike freeway called the Radschnellweg Ruhr.

Rail transport is also vital, with Dortmund's massive hauptbahnhof (main station) being the third largest long-distance rail hub in Germany. High-speed InterCity and Intercity-Express trains connect Dortmund to other major German cities as well as international destinations like Amsterdam, Brussels and Paris.

The city has a light rail system called the Stadtbahn with 8 lines running frequently. Buses supplement the rail network. The unique H-Bahn hanging monorail connects the university campuses.

Dortmund Airport is a medium-sized but fast-growing airport located just east of the city center. It mostly serves low-cost and leisure routes.

Dortmund was ranked as the 7th most livable city for expats in Germany in 2017 and 27th least stressful city in the world. Its transformation from an industrial city to a high-tech hub has been praised.

The city has a long cultural tradition, especially in music and theater. It has one of the largest opera houses in Germany and a renowned concert hall called Konzerthaus Dortmund. The city even has its own acclaimed jazz club.

Other cultural attractions include the U-Tower art center, creative districts like Union Quarter, a famous Christmas market, and abundant parks and gardens like the massive Rombergpark botanical gardens.

There are over 20 museums in Dortmund covering topics like art, cultural history, the region's industrial past, football, and occupational health and safety.

When it comes to sports, Dortmund embraces its nickname as the "City of Sports." It is home to the German Handball Association headquarters as well as many sports clubs and events.

The most famous club is Borussia Dortmund, one of Germany's most successful football teams. Their stadium, Signal Iduna Park, is the largest in Germany with over 81,000 seats and hosted matches during the 2006 World Cup.

In addition to football, Dortmund has professional teams in sports like handball, table tennis, basketball, American football, ice hockey and baseball.

Food? Dortmund has a rich brewing heritage and was formerly known as the "beer capital" of Germany with famous beer brands like Dortmunder Export, Kronen, and Brinkhoffs. Popular local dishes include pfefferpotthast (beef goulash), currywurst (curried sausage), reibekuchen (fried potato pancakes), and the Dortmunder Salzkuchen bread bun.

Dortmund has transformed itself from an industrial city of coal, steel and beer into a modern, high-tech, sustainable city with a vibrant cultural scene and passionate sports following - all while maintaining pride in its industrial roots and brewing heritage. With a lively mix of historical and contemporary attractions alongside abundant green spaces, Dortmund offers an enticing experience for residents and visitors alike in the heart of Germany's Ruhr region.

2.2.1 **Signal Iduna Park**

Signal Iduna Park is a massive football stadium located in Dortmund, Germany. It is the home arena of Borussia Dortmund, one of the top professional clubs in German football. The stadium gets its name from a sponsorship deal with the insurance company Signal Iduna, but is officially called BVB Stadion Dortmund for UEFA competitions. Its original name was

Westfalenstadion, referring to the Westphalia region where Dortmund is situated.

With a total capacity of 81,365 people, Signal Iduna Park is the largest stadium in Germany and the seventh-largest in all of Europe. It can accommodate 65,829 seated spectators for international matches when the standing areas are converted to seats per FIFA rules. The stadium has hosted matches at major tournaments like the 1974 and 2006 FIFA World Cups. It will also be one of the venues for UEFA Euro 2024, holding six matches including a round of 16 game and a semifinal.

The stadium is famous for its intense atmosphere created by passionate Dortmund fans. The south stand, nicknamed "The Yellow Wall," is the largest terrace for standing spectators in European football with a capacity of 25,000. This incredible sea of yellow-clad supporters is known to intimidate even the best opposition players. It has helped Dortmund achieve an unbeaten home record in past Champions League campaigns.

Signal Iduna Park first opened on April 2, 1974, replacing Dortmund's older Stadion Rote Erde. It was originally constructed with a capacity of 54,000 to serve as a venue for that year's World Cup in West Germany. However, the stadium failed to meet FIFA requirements to host semi-final matches, so it had to undergo expansions multiple times over the following decades.

The first major renovation came in 1992 when some standing areas were converted to seating to conform with UEFA regulations, reducing capacity to 42,800. Then in 1995, after Dortmund won the Bundesliga title, second tiers were added to the east and west stands to raise capacity back to 54,000, mostly seated. More expansions followed in 1997 and 1999, culminating in the addition of four new corner sections for the 2006 World Cup that boosted total capacity to 67,000.

The most recent renovations were completed in 2006 to prepare for hosting World Cup matches that year. This included removing old roof supports, adding exterior pylons painted yellow, installing a glass front facade, undersoil heating for winter matches, and four video screens inside the bowl. Capacity was further increased to the current 81,365 total.

The Complete Fan's Companion to EURO 2024

Beyond Borussia Dortmund's Bundesliga home games, Signal Iduna Park has hosted numerous major football events. Six matches were held there during the 2006 World Cup, including Germany's semifinal loss to Italy. The stadium was also the site of the 2001 UEFA Cup final between Liverpool and Alaves. For Euro 2024, it will stage group stage games involving teams like Italy, France, Portugal and Poland in addition to a round of 16 clash and a semifinal.

The stadium offers excellent transportation connections. It has its own train station served by local and regional rail lines, as well as a light rail U-Bahn station at Westfalenhallen just a short walk away. By car, it can be reached via the B1 and B54 highways with parking available nearby.

In the surrounding Kreuzviertel neighborhood, there are many bars, pubs and cafes popular with fans on match days. Here they can enjoy a pre-game beer and bratwurst from street vendors before heading into the iconic Yellow Wall standing section.

While mainly used for football, Signal Iduna Park has hosted a handful of major concerts over the years, though not nearly as many as other big European stadiums. The first concert wasn't held until 2009, a full 35 years after the stadium opened. Altogether, only about 10 concerts have taken place at this famous venue.

Signal Iduna Park truly stands out as one of the great cathedrals of world football. Its imposing size, brilliant modern design, amazing atmosphere created by the Yellow Wall, and historic hosting of huge matches and tournaments have cemented its reputation globally. The stadium has been a big point of pride for the city of Dortmund and the driving force behind Borussia Dortmund's fervent support that opponents have learned to fear. Visiting this iconic venue is an unforgettable experience for any football fan.

There are the matches that will be hosted at Signal Iduna Park for UEFA Euro 2024

On June 15th, 2024, Signal Iduna Park will host its first match of the European Championships as Italy takes on Albania in a Group B contest with kickoff at 9 PM. Three days later on June 18th, the stadium will see Turkey face off against Georgia in Group F at 6 PM. Then on June 22nd,

The Complete Fan's Companion to EURO 2024

Turkey will play their second game at the venue against Portugal, also an 6 PM kickoff in Group F.

The iconic Dortmund arena will next host a Group D clash between heavyweight nations France and Poland on June 25th at 6 PM. Signal Iduna Park's role continues in the knockout rounds as it will stage one of the round of 16 matches on June 29th at 9 PM between the Group A winner and the runner-up from Group C.

The huge stadium will then get the honor of hosting one of the tournament semi-finals on July 10th at 9 PM, where the winners of the two previous quarterfinal matches will battle for a spot in the Euro 2024 final. The teams taking the pitch that night won't be known until after the quarterfinals are completed, but it promises to be a massive spectacle in front of over 80,000 fans at the home of Borussia Dortmund.

2.3 Düsseldorf

Düsseldorf is the capital city of the state of North Rhine-Westphalia in western Germany. It has a population of around 630,000 people. Düsseldorf lies along the Rhine River and is an important center for business, culture, fashion, and the arts.

The city has a very long history dating back centuries, but has grown into a major modern metropolitan area. The name Düsseldorf means "village on the Düssel river." The Düssel branches into several small rivers that flow into the Rhine within the city limits.

The Complete Fan's Companion to EURO 2024

Düsseldorf is considered one of the most livable cities in the world according to some surveys. It attracts many businesses, including being headquarters to major German corporations. The city also hosts important trade fairs and events, especially related to fashion and consumer goods. Around one fifth of the world's premier trade shows are organized in Düsseldorf.

The city has a very vibrant arts and cultural scene. It is home to celebrated art schools like the Kunstakademie Düsseldorf where famous artists like Joseph Beuys taught. There are numerous museums, galleries, theaters, and other cultural institutions located in Düsseldorf. The city hosts annual events like a big Carnival celebration and large Christmas markets that draw many visitors.

Transportation in Düsseldorf is excellent, with a major international airport, train connections, public transit, and highways linking to other cities in the region. The airport is one of the busiest in Germany.

One of Düsseldorf's most famous areas is the Altstadt, the historic Old Town neighborhood. It contains hundreds of bars, breweries, and restaurants concentrated in a small area, earning it the nickname "the longest bar in the world." Drinking the locally-brewed Altbier is very popular in the vibrant Altstadt district.

The Königsallee, or "King's Avenue," is one of Germany's most upscale shopping boulevards. This prestigious street is lined with luxury brands, boutiques, and canal-side cafes. Retail is an important part of Düsseldorf's economy and the city is considered a fashion capital.

Japanese culture has had a big influence in Düsseldorf due to the city's large Japanese population, one of the largest in Europe outside of Japan. There are many Japanese businesses, restaurants, and cultural events and institutions located in Düsseldorf's own "Little Tokyo" area.

The city has many parks and green spaces, including the centrally located Hofgarten which was one of Germany's first public parks when it opened in the 1700s. The Rhine River itself is a major attraction, with a scenic promenade running along the riverfront.

Düsseldorf has a unique architectural mix with historic buildings, modern skyscrapers, and strikingly designed contemporary structures. The Rheinturm tower, with its digital clock display, has become an iconic symbol of the city's skyline at over 800 feet tall. In the harbor area, innovative new architecture by famous architects like Frank Gehry can be found.

Some of Düsseldorf's other top attractions include the Renaissance-era Old Town Hall, Basilica of St. Lambertus church, Maritime Museum, Benrath Palace with its lovely gardens and museum, and the K20 museum housed in a futuristic rounded building showcasing modern art.

Düsseldorf has a friendly rivalry with the nearby city of Cologne. The two cities have competed in many ways, including with their unique local beer cultures - Altbier from Düsseldorf against

Cologne's Kölsch style beer. Residents take great civic pride in their local traditions and accomplishments.

The city hosts many sporting events, teams, and venues. It was one of the German host cities for the 1974 World Cup and will be again for the 2024 European Championships. Düsseldorf is home to successful professional soccer, hockey, basketball, and American football teams among others.

Düsseldorf combines both historic charm and cosmopolitan flair. With its Rhine River setting, world-class cultural activities, lively entertainment districts, upscale shopping and fashion, Japanese influences, and innovative architecture, Düsseldorf offers an exciting experience for travelers to explore and enjoy.

The city manages to blend its long heritage with a modern, global outlook.

2.3.1 Düsseldorf Arena/Merkur Spiel-Arena

The Düsseldorf Arena, also known as the Merkur Spiel-Arena, is a large football stadium located in Düsseldorf, Germany. It has a seating capacity of 54,600 people, with additional standing room that expands the total capacity over 66,000 for concert events.

The arena is the home stadium for the Fortuna Düsseldorf football club. It features a retractable roof that can open or close, allowing events to take place year-round in comfortable conditions thanks to a heating system inside. The stadium's field measures 330 feet by 230 feet.

Construction on the Düsseldorf Arena began in 2002 and was completed in 2004 at a cost of 240 million euros. The stadium was built to replace the older Rheinstadion that previously stood on the same site near the Rhine River. The architectural firm JSK designed the modern arena.

In addition to hosting Fortuna Düsseldorf's home matches, the arena has held several other notable sporting events over the years. It was one of the venues for the 1988 UEFA European Championship, back when it was still called the Rheinstadion. More recently, it hosted matches during the 2024 UEFA European Championship.

The Düsseldorf Arena has been home to other football clubs besides just Fortuna Düsseldorf at times. It was the temporary home stadium for Bayer Leverkusen in 2008-2009 and KFC Uerdingen in 2019-2020 while their own stadiums underwent renovations.

The German national football team played several international friendly matches at the Düsseldorf Arena against opponents like Argentina, Switzerland, Norway, Saudi Arabia and Greece between 2005-2009.

American football was also hosted at the arena for a few years in the mid-2000s, as the Rhein Fire NFL Europe team played their home games there from 2005-2007. The arena hosted theWorld Bowl championship games in 2005 and 2006.

Boxing has found a home at the Düsseldorf Arena as well. Multiple heavyweight championship bouts featuring Wladimir Klitschko took place there, including his 2015 fight against Tyson Fury.

Other sporting events hosted at the arena include the Race of Champions auto racing event in 2010 featuring drivers like Michael Schumacher and Sebastian Vettel. In 2021, it staged the Championship Game for the inaugural European League of Football season.

The arena made headlines in January 2024 by setting a new world record attendance for a handball match. A staggering 53,586 fans packed the Düsseldorf Arena to watch Germany take on

The Complete Fan's Companion to EURO 2024

Switzerland at the European Men's Handball Championship.

Looking ahead, the Düsseldorf Arena will continue hosting major events as it was selected as one of the venues for the 2025 Summer World University Games. It will host the opening ceremony as well as the artistic gymnastics competitions.

Public transportation provides easy access to the Düsseldorf Arena. The Merkur Spiel-Arena/Messe Nord station is located right at the stadium, serving as the terminus for the Line 78 urban rail line that connects to Düsseldorf's public transit system.

Here are the matches the Düsseldorf Arena will host during UEFA EURO 2024:

The Complete Fan's Companion to EURO 2024

The Düsseldorf Arena is set to be one of the venues for the UEFA EURO 2024 football championship. On June 17th, the arena will host its first match of the tournament, a Group D contest between Austria and France kicking off at 9pm. Four days later on June 21st, a Group E match between Slovakia and Ukraine will take place at the arena with a 3pm start time. Then on June 24th, the Düsseldorf Arena will stage a crucial Group B matchup between Albania and Spain under the lights at 9pm. As the knockout rounds begin, the stadium will host a Round of 16 match on July 1st at 6pm between the runners-up from Groups D and E. Finally, the arena has been selected to hold one of the quarter-final matches on July 6th at 6pm, with the winners of two prior Round of 16 matches squaring off for a spot in the semifinals.

The Merkur Spiel-Arena in Düsseldorf is a world-class, multi-purpose stadium that has played host to football matches at the club and international levels, as well as other major sporting events like boxing, American football, auto racing and more. With its modern amenities and accessibility by public transit, it will surely continue attracting big events to Düsseldorf for years to come.

2.4 Frankfurt

Frankfurt is a major metropolitan center in the heart of Germany, situated along the banks of the river Main. With a population of around 770,000 residents, it ranks as the fifth most populous city in the nation. Frankfurt serves as a preeminent global hub for commerce, finance, cultural activities, tourism, and transportation networks.

The city's distinct skyline, adorned with numerous skyscrapers, has earned it the moniker "Mainhattan" - a portmanteau blending the name of the Main River with "Manhattan", alluding to the vertical landscape reminiscent of New York City. Indeed, Frankfurt stands out as one of the few cities within the European Union to boast such an iconic high-rise cityscape. Another nickname, "Bankfurt", underscores its status as a powerhouse in the financial services sector, hosting the headquarters of the European Central Bank along with major banks and financial institutions.

Frankfurt's metropolitan area encompasses over 5.8 million inhabitants, making it the second largest metropolitan region in Germany after the Rhine-Ruhr region. The city exhibits a high degree of cultural diversity, with approximately half of the population having an immigrant background. Around one quarter of Frankfurt's residents are foreign nationals from various countries around the world.

Economically prosperous, Frankfurt ranks among the wealthiest cities globally and stands as Europe's second wealthiest city after London. While frequently lauded for its high quality of living standards, the city also grapples with some of the highest crime rates in Germany, though primarily property offenses rather than violent crimes.

Furthering its role as an international transportation nucleus, Frankfurt hosts one of the world's busiest airports in terms of passenger volume and cargo traffic. The airport boasts its own train stations for long-distance and regional rail services, directly linked to the terminals. Frankfurt's main central railway station is also one of the largest and busiest in Europe.

An extensive public transportation network, consisting of trains, subways, trams, and buses, enables convenient mobility throughout the Frankfurt metropolitan area. Nine S-Bahn commuter train lines connect the city with its surrounding regions, while the U-Bahn subway system operates nine lines as well. Supplementing rail transit is an above-ground tram network and numerous bus routes crisscrossing the city.

Frankfurt takes pride in its abundance of museums, including renowned institutions like the Städel art museum and the museums lining the Museum Embankment along the river Main. The city boasts a vibrant cultural scene, featuring venues such as the acclaimed Frankfurt Opera and the English Theatre – the largest of its kind in continental Europe.

Some of Frankfurt's most iconic landmarks include the Römer, a complex that formerly housed the historic city hall; the Frankfurt Cathedral, where emperors of the Holy Roman Empire were once crowned; the modern Main Tower skyscraper; and the Museumsufer or Museum Embankment, a stretch of museums along the river banks. Complementing the urban landscape are numerous parks and green spaces like the City Forest.

A major destination for global trade fairs and book fairs, Frankfurt annually attracts visitors from around the world. The city has held importance for centuries, previously as a free imperial city and site of imperial coronations during the Holy Roman Empire era. Today, it remains an economic and cultural powerhouse for Germany and Europe as a whole, excelling in sectors like commerce, culture, and transportation networks.

In addition to its commercial and cultural significance, Frankfurt is home to several professional sports teams across various disciplines. The city hosts basketball, American football, Gaelic football, rugby union, and association football (soccer) clubs and franchises that compete at regional, national, and international levels.

Notable among these are the Skyliners Frankfurt basketball team, who claimed the German Basketball Championship in 2004 and the German Cup in 2000. The women's football club 1. FFC Frankfurt, which merged with Eintracht Frankfurt in 2020, holds the record for the most German league titles. Eintracht Frankfurt's men's football team has won the German championship once, clinched the DFB-Pokal (German Cup) five times, and triumphed in the UEFA Cup in 1980 and the Europa League in 2022.

Other prominent sports teams based in Frankfurt include American football franchises Frankfurt

Galaxy and Frankfurt Universe, the Frankfurt Pirates American football club, Frankfurt Sarsfields GAA Gaelic football team, the Löwen Frankfurt ice hockey team, and the rugby union side SC 1880 Frankfurt.

Frankfurt has hosted several major sporting events, including the annual Frankfurt Marathon, the Ironman Germany triathlon competition, and the classic Eschborn-Frankfurt City Loop cycling race, previously known as Rund um den Henninger-Turm from 1961 to 2008. The city is also one of 13 global host locations for the J.P. Morgan Corporate Challenge, Germany's largest corporate sports event.

Beyond the urban core, numerous internationally renowned attractions lie within an 80-kilometer (50-mile) radius of Frankfurt. To the north, visitors can explore the Taunus mountain range, the remnants of the Roman Empire Army Camp Saalburg, and the Limes, the former northern border of the Roman Empire. The towns of Bad Homburg vor der Höhe with its famous casino, Bad Nauheim with its Elvis Presley memorial, and the open-air museum Hessenpark are also popular destinations.

To the west lie the cities of Wiesbaden, renowned for its Kurhaus, State Theater, Neroberg hill, and casino; Rüdesheim; the Rheingau wine region; the Eberbach Monastery, which served as the movie set for the film The Name of the Rose; and the picturesque Rhine Valley along the River Rhine.

Eastward from Frankfurt, visitors can explore the Leather Museum in Offenbach, the city of Hanau which hosts the Grimm Brothers Summer Festival, and the German Fairy Tale Route winding through the Spessart region.

To the south, points of interest include the city of Darmstadt with its Art Nouveau Mathildenhöhe district, the Waldspirale (Forest Spiral) residential building, the former private chapel of the last Tsar of Russia, the Vortex Garden, the Odenwald range, the Bergstrasse region, the vineyards of Heppenheim, and the historic Frankenstein Castle.

With its blend of economic prowess, cultural vibrancy, transportation connectivity, sporting activities, and proximity to numerous attractions, Frankfurt positions itself as a great destination catering to an array of interests for visitors and residents alike.

2.4.1 **Deutsche Bank Park**

The Deutsche Bank Park, previously known as the Waldstadion (Forest Stadium), is an iconic sports stadium located in Frankfurt, Germany. It serves as the home ground for the football club Eintracht Frankfurt. The stadium has a rich history dating back to 1925 when it was originally opened after four years of construction at a cost of 3.7 million marks (equivalent to €14 million today).

The initial stadium had a capacity of 35,000 spectators, with the grandstands primarily consisting of earthworks, except for the north side, which was made of reinforced concrete and modeled after an ancient Greek theater. The

Waldstadion hosted its first major national event, the final of the German football championship, in 1925, where 1. FC Nürnberg defeated local club FSV Frankfurt 1-0.

Over the years, the stadium underwent several renovations and expansions to increase its capacity and meet the requirements of hosting major international tournaments. In 1937, the capacity was increased to 55,000 through the expansion of the back straight.

The first significant modification took place in 1955 after a game between Eintracht Frankfurt and 1. FC Nürnberg in 1953, where nearly 70,000 tickets were sold for a stadium designed for only 55,000 spectators, leading to injuries as thousands tried to force entry. The renovated and enlarged Waldstadion was reopened after 19 months of construction work.

In preparation for the 1974 FIFA World Cup, the stadium underwent a second major renovation from May 1972 to January 1974, virtually rebuilding it from scratch to meet the comfort and safety requirements of the World Cup venues. The opening ceremony of the 1974 World Cup was held at the Waldstadion.

The most recent redevelopment of the stadium took place in 2005, transforming it into a football-only stadium in preparation for the 2005 FIFA Confederations Cup and the 2006 FIFA World Cup. The stadium was renamed the Commerzbank-Arena during this period and underwent a €150 million renovation by architects

Gerkan, Marg and Partners, and Max Bögl.

The current Deutsche Bank Park has a capacity of 58,000 spectators for league matches, making it the seventh-largest football stadium in Germany. It has hosted numerous prestigious international tournaments, including the 1974 FIFA World Cup, UEFA Euro 1988, the 2005 FIFA Confederations Cup, the 2006 FIFA World Cup, and the 2011 FIFA Women's World Cup, where it hosted the final.

In the upcoming UEFA Euro 2024, the Deutsche Bank Park will host five matches, including:

1. June 17, 2024, 18:00 CET: Belgium vs. Slovakia (Group E)
2. June 20, 2024, 18:00 CET: Denmark vs. England (Group C)

The Complete Fan's Companion to EURO 2024

3. June 23, 2024, 21:00 CET: Switzerland vs. Germany (Group A)

4. June 26, 2024, 18:00 CET: Slovakia vs. Romania (Group E)

5. July 1, 2024, 21:00 CET: Round of 16 match – Winner Group F vs. 3rd-placed team from Groups A/B/C

The stadium complex, owned by the city of Frankfurt, includes not only the main arena but also other sports facilities such as a swimming pool, tennis complex, beach volleyball court, and a winter sports hall. It has its own railway station, Frankfurt Stadion, on the national rail network, making it easily accessible for spectators.

In 2023, the Deutsche Bank Park hosted two regular season National Football League (NFL)

American football games as part of the NFL Germany Games, showcasing its versatility in hosting different sporting events.

2.5 **Gelsenkirchen**

Gelsenkirchen is a significant city located in the state of North Rhine-Westphalia, Germany. With a population of 262,528 (as of 2016), it is the 25th most populous city in Germany and the 11th largest in the state of North Rhine-Westphalia. Situated on the Emscher River, a tributary of the Rhine, Gelsenkirchen lies at the center of the Ruhr region, which is the largest urban area in Germany. It is the fifth largest city in Westphalia after Dortmund, Bochum, Bielefeld, and Münster, and is one of the southernmost cities in the Low German dialect area.

Gelsenkirchen is renowned for its association with the football club Schalke 04, which is named after the Gelsenkirchen-Schalke district. However, the club's current stadium, the Veltins-Arena, is located in the Gelsenkirchen-Erle district. The city has a rich industrial heritage, particularly in coal mining and heavy industry, but has diversified its economy in recent times.

Gelsenkirchen presents itself as a center of solar technology, with companies like Shell Solar Deutschland GmbH producing solar cells in the Rotthausen area and Scheuten Solar Technology taking over solar panel production. Other notable businesses in the city include THS Wohnen, Gelsenwasser, e.on, BP Gelsenkirchen GmbH, and Pilkington. Additionally, the ZOOM

The Complete Fan's Companion to EURO 2024

Erlebniswelt Gelsenkirchen, a zoo founded in 1949 as "Ruhr-Zoo," is operated by the city.

In terms of transportation, Gelsenkirchen is well-connected, lying on the autobahns A2, A40, A42, and A52, as well as the federal highways B224, B226, and B227. The city's central station, Gelsenkirchen Hauptbahnhof, is situated at the junction of the Duisburg–Dortmund, Essen–Gelsenkirchen, and Gelsenkirchen–Münster railway lines. The Rhine-Herne Canal also has a commercial-industrial harbor in Gelsenkirchen, known as Gelsenkirchen Harbour, which is one of the biggest and most important canal harbors in Germany, with a yearly turnover of 2 million tonnes and a water surface area of about 1.2 square kilometers.

Local transport in Gelsenkirchen is provided by the Bochum/Gelsenkirchen tramway network, buses run by the Bochum-Gelsenkirchener Straßenbahn AG (BOGESTRA), and buses operated by Vestische Straßenbahnen GmbH in the city's north. There are three tram lines, one light rail line, and about 50 bus routes in Gelsenkirchen, all integrated into the VRR fare structure.

Gelsenkirchen is also known for its sports heritage, particularly in football. The city is home to the football club FC Schalke 04, currently playing in the 2. Bundesliga, the second tier of German football. The club has won 7 Bundesliga titles, and their home ground, the Arena AufSchalke, was one of the venues that hosted matches during the 2006 FIFA World Cup. Several famous German football players and managers, including İlkay Gündoğan, Mesut Özil, Olaf Thon, Manuel Neuer, and Michael Skibbe, were born in Gelsenkirchen. Additionally, the city has a harness racing track, the Trabrennbahn Gelsenkirchen, which has been operational since 1912.

2.5.1 **Veltins-Arena**

The Arena AufSchalke, currently known as the Veltins-Arena for sponsorship reasons, is an iconic retractable roof football stadium located in Gelsenkirchen, North Rhine-Westphalia, Germany. It serves as the home ground for the renowned football club FC Schalke 04, one of the most successful traditional clubs in Germany with seven Bundesliga titles and the 1996/97 UEFA Cup winners.

The stadium opened its doors on August 13, 2001, replacing the outdated Parkstadion, which was Schalke 04's previous home. The construction of the Veltins-Arena was a significant milestone for the club, as it not only provided a modern and multifunctional arena but also aligned with their upcoming 100th anniversary in 2004 and their historic UEFA Cup victory in 1997.

The Veltins-Arena boasts an impressive capacity of 62,271 for league matches, with standing and seated areas. However, for international matches, the capacity is reduced to 54,740, with all seats being in a seated configuration. This versatility allows the stadium to cater to different match requirements and regulations.

One of the standout features of the Veltins-Arena is its retractable roof and slide-out pitch. The Teflon-coated fiberglass canvas retractable roof spans the entire stadium, supported by a rectangular truss suspended above the field and connected to the main building via 24 steel pylons. The center of the roof can be opened into two halves, allowing for an open or covered stadium, depending on weather conditions and event requirements.

The slide-out pitch is another remarkable engineering feat. Supported by an 11,400-tonne substructure, the playing field can be moved in and out of the stadium within four hours. This feature offers several advantages, including allowing the grass surface to grow under normal outdoor conditions without suffering from lack of circulation and light, preventing damage to the pitch during indoor events like concerts, and enabling the conversion of the multi-functional hall within a short amount of time.

The stadium's design and layout were carefully planned to accommodate the presence of two mine shafts running beneath the site at a depth of 800 meters. To avoid potential structural issues, the main axis of the stadium was rotated from the classic north-south arrangement to a northeast-southwest alignment, making it parallel to the mine shafts.

The Veltins-Arena features two tiers that completely surround the playing field, providing excellent sightlines for spectators. The North stand is dedicated to standing rows for Schalke 04 fans during league matches, with a capacity of 16,307. For international matches, these standing rows are converted into seats, reducing the capacity to 8,600. Additionally, the stadium features 72 VIP lounges that form a ring around the entire structure, separating the first tier from the second tier.

The stadium's versatility and state-of-the-art facilities have enabled it to host numerous high-profile events. In 2004, it hosted the UEFA Champions League Final, showcasing its ability to stage major international tournaments. During the renovation of the Rheinstadion in Düsseldorf, the Veltins-Arena served as a temporary home for the Rhein Fire of NFL Europe, an American football league, and hosted World Bowl XII.

The 2006 FIFA World Cup was another major event held at the Veltins-Arena, then officially known as the FIFA World Cup Stadium

Gelsenkirchen due to FIFA's sponsorship regulations. It hosted five matches during the tournament, including a quarterfinal clash between England and Portugal, where Wayne Rooney was infamously sent off.

In addition to football, the Veltins-Arena has hosted a variety of other sporting events, such as the biathlon World Team Challenge exhibition race, stock car races, operas, and even a world heavyweight championship boxing match between Wladimir Klitschko and Ruslan Chagaev in 2009, which drew an audience of 60,000 spectators.

One of the most remarkable events hosted at the Veltins-Arena was the opening game of the 74th IIHF Ice Hockey World Championship in 2010. On this occasion, the stadium set a world record for ice hockey attendance, with a staggering crowd of 77,803 spectators witnessing the host team Germany defeat the United States 2-1 in overtime.

In 2018, the Veltins-Arena made history in a different sport by hosting the German Darts Masters, which achieved a record-breaking attendance of 20,210 spectators, the highest ever for a darts event. The tournament was won by Mensur Suljović.

Looking ahead, the Veltins-Arena will continue to play a significant role in hosting major international tournaments. In 2024, it will be one of the venues for the UEFA Euro 2024 tournament, hosting four matches:

The Complete Fan's Companion to EURO 2024

1. June 16, 2024, 21:00 CEST: Serbia vs. England (Group C)
2. June 20, 2024, 21:00 CEST: Spain vs. Italy (Group B)
3. June 26, 2024, 21:00 CEST: Georgia vs. Portugal (Group F)
4. June 30, 2024, 18:00 CEST: Round of 16 match – Winner of Group C vs. 3rd-placed team from Groups D/E/F

However, due to sponsorship contracts, the arena will use its non-sponsored name, Arena AufSchalke, during the UEFA Euro 2024 tournament.

The Veltins-Arena has also expressed its intention to bid for hosting one of the UEFA Europa League finals or a UEFA Women's Champions League final in either 2026 or 2027, further solidifying its status as a premier venue for international football competitions.

Beyond its remarkable sporting events and facilities, the Veltins-Arena holds significant historical and cultural significance for the city of Gelsenkirchen and the Ruhr region. As the home of FC Schalke 04, one of the most beloved and successful football clubs in Germany, the stadium has become an integral part of the local community's identity and a source of pride for generations of fans.

With its state-of-the-art design, innovative engineering, and ability to host a wide range of events, the Veltins-Arena (Arena AufSchalke) is Germany's commitment to providing world-class sports and entertainment facilities.

2.6 **Hamburg**

Hamburg is a major port city in northern Germany. It is the second largest city in the country after Berlin and the 8th largest city in the European Union, with a population of over 1.9 million people. The larger Hamburg Metropolitan Region has over 5.1 million inhabitants.

Hamburg has a long history going back to the medieval era. It was an important trading center as part of the Hanseatic League and a free imperial city of the Holy Roman Empire. Before German unification in 1871, Hamburg was a fully sovereign city-state. After overcoming disasters like the Great Fire, floods, and bombing raids during World War II, Hamburg recovered and emerged wealthier each time.

Today, Hamburg is one of Germany's 16 federal states. It has a strong economy and is an important media, commercial, logistical and industrial hub. Major companies headquartered here include Airbus, Blohm+Voss, Aurubis, Beiersdorf, Lufthansa and Unilever. The port is the third largest in Europe after Rotterdam and Antwerp.

Hamburg is home to research institutions like the Deutsches Elektronen-Synchrotron Laboratory DESY. It hosts international organizations focused on areas such as maritime law, education, and political cooperation between Europe, Latin America and China. Two former German chancellors - Helmut Schmidt and Angela Merkel - were born in Hamburg, as was the current chancellor Olaf Scholz.

Tourism is another major part of Hamburg's economy, with almost 7 million overnight visitor stays in 2017. Major attractions include the Speicherstadt and Kontorhausviertel warehouse districts, which are UNESCO World Heritage sites. Hamburg has around 2,500 bridges - more than Venice, Amsterdam and London combined. It also has the highest number of churches over 100 meters tall of any city worldwide.

Other major sights are the modern Elbphilharmonie concert hall, the St. Pauli nightlife district including the famous Reeperbahn, and the Miniatur Wunderland - the world's largest model railway museum. Hamburg was the birthplace of the famous Beatles music group.

The city features a mix of modern and historical architecture styles. In addition to churches, other prominent buildings include the neo-Renaissance Town Hall, the Chilehaus office building in the Brick Expressionist style, and newly developed areas like the HafenCity district.

Hamburg has an oceanic climate influenced by its proximity to the sea. Winters are cool with occasional snowfall, while summers are mild. The nearby Alster river has been dammed to create two lakes in the city center.

While German is the predominant language, many people speak Standard German rather than the local Missingsch dialect, though some vocabulary and street names reflect it. Around a quarter of residents are Protestant and 10% are

Catholic, with Muslims making up a sizable minority as well.

Food and drink are an important part of Hamburg's culture. Typical dishes feature fish like soused herrings, fried plaice, smoked eel and carp. Other specialties include labskaus (a beef and root vegetable stew), birnen, bohnen und speck (pears, green beans and bacon), and franzbrotchen pastries. Locally brewed beers have been famous exports since the Middle Ages.

Sports are also very popular in Hamburg. The city's two biggest football clubs are Hamburger SV and FC St. Pauli. Hamburg also hosts major annual events like the German Open tennis tournament, horse racing derbies, the Hamburg Marathon, and cycling competitions. It made an unsuccessful bid for the 2024 Summer Olympics.

In terms of infrastructure, Hamburg has a modern transportation network of roads, railways and airports including the fifth largest airport in Germany. Over 30 rail transit lines and extensive bus services enable public transportation around the city. Ferry lines cross the Elbe river.

Hamburg combines its heritage as an historic trading powerhouse with modern development as a center for business, media, research, tourism and culture in northern Germany. Its maritime spirit lives on in its port facilities, merchant shipping, and seafaring traditions. With its green spaces and water territories, Hamburg offers an appealing quality of life within an economically prosperous European metropolis.

2.6.1 **Volksparkstadion**

The Volksparkstadion is a football stadium located in Hamburg, Germany. It is the home ground of Hamburger SV football club. The stadium has a capacity of 49,000 for matchday crowds.

The current Volksparkstadion first opened its doors in 1953, but it underwent a major renovation and upgrade in 2000. This transformed it into a modern stadium properly suited for hosting top-level football matches. Despite its recent renovation, the stadium has a long history of hosting major football events.

In 1974, the Volksparkstadion was one of the venues used for that year's FIFA World Cup held in West Germany. It hosted three group stage matches during the tournament. The first saw East Germany defeat Australia 2-1 in front of just 17,000 fans. But the crowds grew for the next two matches as hosts West Germany took to the field, with 53,300 attending their 3-0 win over Australia and 60,200 packing in to see their 0-1 loss to East Germany.

The stadium was also a venue for the 1988 European Championship, staging the semi-final between West Germany and the Netherlands. The Dutch won that match 2-1 to advance to the final.

The Volksparkstadion was one of the stadiums used for the 2006 FIFA World Cup hosted in

Germany. During that tournament, it hosted four group stage games and one quarter-final match under the temporary name of FIFA World Cup Stadium Hamburg due to sponsorship deals.

In 2010, the stadium was the site of that year's UEFA Europa League final between Atlético Madrid and Fulham, with Atlético claiming a 2-1 victory.

Looking ahead, the Volksparkstadion will be one of the venues for the 2024 European Championship scheduled to take place in Germany. It will host five matches during the tournament - four group stage games and one quarter-final.

The opening group match in Hamburg will see Poland take on the Netherlands on June 16th,

2024 at 3pm local time. Three days later on June 19th, Croatia will face Albania at 3pm. Georgia and the Czech Republic will then meet on June 22nd at 3pm. Finally, the Czech Republic will play Turkey in a 9pm kick-off on June 26th to wrap up the group stage action in Hamburg. The stadium's fifth and final Euro 2024 match will be a quarter-final tie on July 5th at 9pm.

In addition to its rich history of hosting major football events, the Volksparkstadion has also staged some other notable sporting and entertainment events over the years. This includes a heavyweight unification boxing match between Wladimir Klitschko and David Haye in 2011 that Klitschko won by unanimous decision in front of a sold-out crowd.

The stadium has also been a popular concert venue, hosting major acts like Michael Jackson, Tina Turner, Depeche Mode, Metallica, AC/DC, Coldplay, Rihanna, P!nk, Beyoncé, The Weeknd and more. Taylor Swift is even scheduled to bring her Eras Tour to the Volksparkstadion for two shows in July 2024.

For transport, the stadium is easily accessible by rail, with the Stellingen station on the Hamburg S-Bahn network being the closest stop. Free shuttle bus services are provided from Stellingen and Othmarschen stations for major events. The A7 Autobahn also runs nearby for those driving, though parking at the stadium itself is extremely limited.

The Volksparkstadion is a modern stadium with an illustrious history of hosting some of football's biggest events. Its great location and amenities make it an ideal venue that will surely continue attracting more marquee matches, concerts and happenings in the years ahead.

2.7 **Cologne**

Cologne is a major city located in western Germany, situated along the banks of the Rhine River. It has a population of over 1 million residents within the city limits, making it the fourth largest city in Germany. The wider Cologne-Bonn metropolitan area is home to around 3.5 million people.

Cologne traces its origins way back to being established as a Roman colony in the 1st century AD. Known then as Colonia Agrippina, it served as an important regional capital for the Romans. The city's name evolved from this starting point, going from Colonia to its current German name of Köln and the English name of Cologne over the centuries. Cologne remained an influential city through the Middle Ages as a member of the Hanseatic trading league.

The city has a long history as an important center for Christianity in Europe. Cologne Cathedral is the city's most iconic landmark and biggest tourist attraction. Construction began on this grand Gothic cathedral back in 1248, with it finally being completed in 1880. The 515 foot tall structure was the world's tallest building from 1880 to 1890. The cathedral is also notable for housing the Shrine of the Three Kings, which reputedly contains the remains of the Three Wise Men from the Bible.

In addition to the cathedral, Cologne boasts 11 other major Romanesque churches dating back to medieval times. Incredibly, all 12 of these churches suffered heavy damage during World War II but have since been restored or reconstructed.

Like much of Germany's industrial heartland, Cologne was heavily bombed by Allied forces during the war. By the end of the conflict in 1945, an astounding 95% of the city center lay in ruins. The rebuilding effort made preservation of historic buildings a priority where possible, but also led to a very modern style of architecture being integrated into Cologne's city center.

Some of Cologne's other top attractions and architecture highlights include the Cologne City

Hall, which dates back to the 12th century and is the oldest city hall in Germany still in operation. The 15th century Overstolzenhaus is another superb example of medieval architecture. And while most of Cologne's old city gates were destroyed in the war, the Eigelsteintor, Hahnentorburg, and Severinstorburg gates still remain intact. Notable churches beyond the famous cathedral include Great St. Martin, St. Severin, and the Church of the Assumption.

Cologne's location along the Rhine River has been key to its prosperity over the centuries as a major trading center and transportation hub. Several bridges cross the river, with the Hohenzollern Bridge being an iconic structure. Cologne also has a major port that ranks as one of the largest inland ports in Germany and all of Europe.

When it comes to modern architecture in Cologne, one of the most distinct skyscrapers is the Colonius telecommunications tower that stands 873 feet tall. Other tall buildings making up Cologne's skyline include the Colonia-Hochhaus at 482 feet, Rheintower at 453 feet, Uni-Center at 436 feet, and KölnTriangle at 338 feet tall.

In terms of culture and arts, Cologne has a rich offering with over 30 museums and hundreds of art galleries. The Museum Ludwig boasts one of the most comprehensive modern art collections in all of Europe, including many works by Picasso. Meanwhile, the Roman-Germanic Museum highlights artifacts excavated in Cologne from ancient Roman times.

Cologne also has a vibrant music scene, being home to the Gürzenich and WDR Symphony Orchestras, and formerly the influential electronic music studio of Karlheinz Stockhausen. The city hosts major annual festivals showcasing literature, philosophy, and of course, the famous Cologne Carnival celebration each spring.

The centuries-old Cologne Carnival is one of the biggest street festivals in Europe. The crazy Carnival season officially begins each year on November 11 at 11:11am and continues until Ash Wednesday, with the peak celebrations happening in the week beforehand. Hundreds of thousands of people take to the streets in costume to celebrate.

Cologne and its neighboring city of Düsseldorf have cultivated a fierce but jovial rivalry over the years. This extends from competition between their respective Carnival celebrations and football clubs to a battle of the brands over the local beer styles of Kölsch in Cologne and Altbier in Düsseldorf.

Beer certainly plays a major role in Cologne's culture and culinary identity. Kölsch is not just the local dialect, but also the name of the city's iconic filtered beer which dates back to the early 1800s. Several big breweries like Reissdorf and Gaffel operate in Cologne producing this coveted beer style.

On the subject of food and drink traditions, Cologne is also renowned as the birthplace of Eau de Cologne, a distinctive perfume created by an Italian immigrant in the early 18th century. Two companies - one from the original Farina family, and the other the famous 4711 brand - still produce authentic Eau de Cologne in the city using traditional methods.

Looking at Cologne's economy and business, it is one of the most important economic centers in the Rhine-Ruhr metropolitan region, which has immense industrial output. Major companies headquartered in Cologne include the insurance giants Rewe Group and Zurich, German media conglomerate RTL, and the European Aviation Safety Agency.

Global transportation and logistics is another key industry for Cologne. The city has its own major international airport as well as extensive rail, road, and river port infrastructure connecting it to destinations across Europe. Automobile manufacturing is represented by a major Ford factory in the Cologne district of Niehl, while Toyota's high-performance motorsports division is headquartered in Marsdorf.

In recent years, Cologne has emerged as one of Germany's most important start-up hubs, especially for digital and tech-focused companies. The city was also the first in Germany with over 1 million residents to declare a climate emergency, underscoring its commitment to sustainable urban policies.

Beyond its economic clout, Cologne is a major center for higher education and research. It is home to the renowned University of Cologne which dates back to 1388, making it one of the oldest universities in Europe. Cologne is also home to the prestigious German Sport University, three Max Planck research institutes, and the German Aerospace Center.

As for sports, Cologne has professional clubs in football (1. FC Köln), ice hockey (Kölner Haie), and other sports. The city's football stadium RheinEnergieStadion hosted matches during the 2006 FIFA World Cup. Cologne also has a storied history in other sports like rowing, cycling, golf, boxing, and track and field.

Cologne stands out as a city that perfectly blends its deep historical roots and cultural heritage with thoroughly modern urban development and economic progress. From its awe-inspiring cathedral to its raucous Carnival celebrations and world-famous beer, Cologne proudly preserves its unique local traditions. At the same time, it has emerged as an influential player in industries like media, insurance, transportation, manufacturing, and technology for the 21st century.

2.7.1 **RheinEnergieStadion**

The RheinEnergieStadion, formerly known as the Müngersdorfer Stadion, is a large football stadium located in Cologne, Germany. It has a capacity of 50,000 for regular matches involving its home team 1. FC Köln, who compete in the top level Bundesliga.

The stadium first opened in 1923 after the city was allowed to construct new buildings on land previously occupied by fortifications under the Treaty of Versailles after World War I. Building the original Müngersdorfer Stadion was an important project that created 15,000 jobs for Cologne during an economic downturn. The initial construction cost over 47 million marks.

Over the following decades, the Müngersdorfer Stadion hosted many memorable matches and events. The German national team made their first appearance at the ground in November 1927, drawing 2-2 with the Netherlands. It went on to be the site of 19 more German national team games up until renovations in the 2000s. Other highlights included the first big post-war match in 1948, which saw a crowd of 75,000.

In the 1970s, Cologne began exploring plans to build an entirely new 80,000-seat stadium to host matches for the 1974 World Cup. However, the project ended up being too expensive at over

93 million marks. Instead, renovations were made to the Müngersdorfer Stadion from 1972-1975 to increase capacity to 61,000. This updated version of the stadium was able to host games at the 1988 European Championship.

As Germany prepared to host the 2006 World Cup, another major renovation was undertaken from 2002-2004 at a cost of 117 million euros. This time, the running track was removed and spectators were brought much closer to the playing field in a bowl design. The stadium's most distinctive new feature was four large illuminated corner towers.

When it reopened in 2004, the renovated stadium was known as the FIFA World Cup Stadium Cologne for that year's Confederations Cup matches and the 2006 World Cup games it hosted. Five matches were played there during the 2006 World Cup, including group stage clashes between Portugal-Angola, Czech Republic-Ghana, Sweden-England, Togo-France, and a Round of 16 match between Switzerland and Ukraine.

Following the World Cup, the stadium received its current name of the RheinEnergieStadion through a naming rights deal with the local energy company RheinEnergie AG. As the home of 1. FC Köln, it has also hosted many important cup matches over the years involving German and other European clubs like Bayer Leverkusen, Barcelona, Monaco, Arsenal and more.

More recently, the RheinEnergieStadion was the venue for the 2020 UEFA Europa League final between Sevilla and Inter Milan. This match was originally scheduled for Gdansk, Poland but was moved to Cologne and played behind closed doors due to the COVID-19 pandemic. Sevilla defeated Inter 3-2 to claim the title.

Looking ahead, the RheinEnergieStadion will serve as one of the venues for the 2024 European Championship being hosted across Germany. During that tournament, the stadium will officially be referred to as Cologne Stadium per UEFA sponsorship rules. It is scheduled to host five matches in total - four group stage games and one Round of 16 clash.

The group stage action will see the stadium welcome Hungary vs Switzerland on June 15th, Scotland vs Switzerland on June 19th, Belgium vs Romania on June 22nd, and England vs Slovenia on June 25th. Then on June 30th, Cologne

Stadium will stage a Round of 16 knockout matchup featuring the winner of Group B against the third-place team from either Group A, D, E or F.

When it comes to facilities, the RheinEnergieStadion features a standard FIFA-approved playing field of 105 x 68 meters. For international matches, capacity is reduced slightly to 45,965 as terracing areas cannot be used. The entire pitch has floodlights installed, and the north grandstand contains a museum dedicated to 1. FC Köln.

The stadium has exterior dimensions of 220 meters long by 180 meters wide, with a roof height of 33.25 meters covering an area of 15,400 square meters. Architecturally, the stadium was designed by Gerkan, Marg und Partner, with

Schlaich Bergermann & Partner serving as structural engineers.

The RheinEnergieStadion forms part of the larger Sportpark Müngersdorf complex next to Aachener Strasse in western Cologne. It can be accessed by car via the Cologne ring road Bundesautobahn 1, or by rail on the Cologne Stadtbahn system at the appropriately named RheinEnergieStadion station.

In 2004, the stadium was awarded a bronze medal as a distinguished sporting and leisure facility by the International Olympic Committee. So in addition to serving as the home of 1. FC Köln and a venue for international soccer matches, it is also used for other sporting events and major concerts by international music acts.

Some notable concerts that have taken place at the RheinEnergieStadion over the years include performances by Tina Turner during her wildly popular 1990s tours, as well as more recent shows by Rihanna in 2016 and P!nk in 2019 as part of their respective world tours.

While the RheinEnergieStadion is most famous for hosting soccer matches involving the German national team, World Cup, and 1. FC Köln, it has also been home to other sports clubs and teams based in Cologne throughout its century-long history.

In the early years from 1923 to 1947, the original Müngersdorfer Stadion served as home grounds for local football clubs Kölner BC 01 and SpVgg Sülz 07. More recently from 2004 to 2007, the Cologne Centurions American football team played their home games at the stadium. And lower-division Cologne soccer club Viktoria Koln continues to use the RheinEnergieStadion for selected high-profile matches.

The RheinEnergieStadion is not just the home of 1. FC Köln and one of Germany's most prominent soccer cathedrals. Over the past century since first opening in 1923, this stadium has been renovated and expanded multiple times to keep up with modern facility standards. It has hosted numerous major soccer tournaments and other marquee events, instantly recognizable for its illuminated corner towers and lively atmosphere. And looking ahead, the RheinEnergieStadion seems poised to continue attracting more of the biggest games and occasions as a proud ambassador for German football and the city of Cologne.

2.8 **Leipzig**

Leipzig is a city in the German state of Saxony. It is the most populous city in Saxony and the eighth most populous city in Germany. Leipzig has a population of around 628,718 inhabitants as of 2023.

The name of the city and its districts has Slavic origins. Leipzig is located about 150 km southwest of Berlin, in the southernmost part of the North German Plain, at the confluence of the White Elster and its tributaries Pleiße and Parthe. These rivers form an extensive inland delta in the city known as the "Leipziger Gewässerknoten". Leipzig is situated at the center of Neuseenland, an area consisting of several artificial lakes created from former lignite open-pit mines.

Leipzig has been a trade city since the time of the Holy Roman Empire. The city sits at the intersection of the Via Regia and the Via Imperii, two important medieval trade routes. Leipzig's trade fair dates back to 1190. Between 1764 and 1945, the city was a center of publishing. After the Second World War and during the period of the German Democratic Republic (East Germany), Leipzig remained a major urban center, but its cultural and economic importance declined.

Events in Leipzig in 1989 played a significant role in precipitating the fall of communism in Central and Eastern Europe, mainly through demonstrations starting from St. Nicholas Church. The immediate effects of the reunification of Germany included the collapse of the local economy, severe unemployment, and urban blight. By the early 2000s, the trend had reversed, and Leipzig underwent significant changes, including urban and economic rejuvenation, and modernization of the transport infrastructure.

Leipzig is home to one of the oldest universities in Europe, the University of Leipzig. It is also the main seat of the German National Library, the seat of the German Music Archive, and the German Federal Administrative Court. Leipzig Zoo is one of the most modern zoos in Europe and ranks first in Germany and second in Europe as of 2018.

Leipzig's Gründerzeit architecture consists of around 12,500 buildings. The city's central railway terminus, Leipzig Hauptbahnhof, is

Europe's largest railway station measured by floor area. Since the Leipzig City Tunnel came into operation in 2013, it has formed the centerpiece of the S-Bahn Mitteldeutschland, Germany's largest S-Bahn network.

Leipzig has long been a major center for music, including classical and modern dark wave. The Thomanerchor, a boys' choir, was founded in 1212. The Leipzig Gewandhaus Orchestra, established in 1743, is one of the oldest symphony orchestras in the world. Several well-known composers lived and worked in Leipzig, including Johann Sebastian Bach and Felix Mendelssohn.

The city's name, Leipzig, is ultimately derived from the Slavic designation for basswood or lime trees. In 1937, the Nazi government officially renamed the city Reichsmessestadt Leipzig

(Reich Trade Fair City Leipzig). In 1989, Leipzig was dubbed a "Hero City", alluding to the honorary title awarded in the former Soviet Union to certain cities that played a key role in the victory of the Allies during the Second World War, in recognition of the role that the Monday demonstrations there played in the fall of the East German regime.

Leipzig is located in the Leipzig Bay, the southernmost part of the North German Plain. The city sits on the White Elster, a river that rises in the Czech Republic and flows into the Saale south of Halle. The landscape is mostly flat, though there is also some evidence of moraine and drumlins.

Since 1992, Leipzig has been divided administratively into ten boroughs, which contain a total of 63 localities. Some of these correspond to outlying villages which have been annexed by Leipzig.

Leipzig is well known for its large parks, including the Leipziger Auwald (riparian forest) and Neuseenland, an area south of Leipzig where old open-cast mines are being converted into a huge lake district. Leipzig Botanical Garden is the oldest of its kind in Germany.

Leipzig has long been a major center for music, including classical and modern dark wave. The Thomanerchor, a boys' choir, was founded in 1212. The Leipzig Gewandhaus Orchestra, established in 1743, is one of the oldest symphony orchestras in the world. Several well-known composers lived and worked in Leipzig, including Johann Sebastian Bach and Felix Mendelssohn.

Leipzig is known for its independent music scene and subcultural events. The Wave-Gotik-Treffen, currently the world's largest Gothic festival, has been held in Leipzig for thirty years.

Leipzig hosts several annual events, including the Auto Mobil International motor show, the AMITEC trade fair for vehicle maintenance, the Bachfest (Johann Sebastian Bach festival), the Leipzig Christmas Market (since 1458), the Dok Leipzig international festival for documentary and animated film, and the Wave-Gotik-Treffen at Pentecost.

Local dishes in Leipzig include Leipziger Allerlei, a stew consisting of seasonal vegetables and crayfish, and Leipziger Lerche, a shortcrust pastry dish filled with crushed almonds, nuts, and strawberry jam. Gose is a locally brewed top-fermenting sour beer that originated in the Goslar region and became popular in 18th-century Leipzig.

Leipzig has more than 250 sport clubs, representing about 80 different disciplines. The city was the venue for the 2006 FIFA World Cup draw and hosted several matches during the tournament. RB Leipzig, a football club that came up through the ranks of German football and gained promotion to the Bundesliga in 2016, won the DFB-Pokal football cup in 2022 and 2023.

Leipzig is a location for automobile manufacturing by BMW and Porsche in large plants north of the city. DHL transferred the bulk of its European air operations from Brussels Airport to Leipzig/Halle Airport in 2011 and 2012.

The city also houses the European Energy Exchange, the leading energy exchange in Central Europe.

Leipzig benefits from world-leading medical research and a growing biotechnology industry. Many bars, restaurants, and stores in the downtown area are patronized by German and foreign tourists. Leipzig is one of Germany's most visited cities, with over 3 million overnight stays in 2017.

Leipzig has been ranked as one of the most livable cities in Germany, with an attractive inner city, vibrant gastronomy, and shopping opportunities. The city has also been recognized for its future prospects and dynamic economic growth.

Leipzig has an extensive transport infrastructure, including railways, trams, buses, and bicycle-friendly routes. Leipzig Hauptbahnhof is the main hub of the tram and railway network and the world's largest railway station by floor area. The city is also served by Leipzig/Halle Airport, an international commercial airport and a major cargo hub.

2.7.1 **Red Bull Arena**

The Red Bull Arena is the home stadium of RB Leipzig, a football club based in Leipzig, Germany. RB Leipzig has been playing its home matches at the Red Bull Arena since 2010, and the stadium has witnessed many great moments for the club, with more to come in the future.

The Red Bull Arena was constructed in the year 2000 and officially opened on July 16-17, 2004. It has a maximum capacity of 47,069 spectators, making it a sizable and impressive venue for hosting football matches.

Since 2010, the Red Bull Arena has been the living room for RB Leipzig, a club that has rapidly risen through the ranks of German football. RB Leipzig was formed in 2009 after Red Bull took over a local 5th division football club, SSV Markranstädt. The club was renamed RB Leipzig and began its journey through the lower leagues of German football.

Over the years, RB Leipzig has achieved remarkable success, culminating in their promotion to the Bundesliga, the top division of German football, in 2016. The Red Bull Arena has been the home ground for RB Leipzig throughout this journey, witnessing the club's ascent to the highest level of the game.

The Red Bull Arena has hosted many memorable moments for RB Leipzig and its passionate fans. The stadium has been the stage for crucial matches, victories, and celebrations as the club established itself as a force to be reckoned with in German football.

One of the standout achievements for RB Leipzig was winning the DFB-Pokal, the German football cup, in 2022 and 2023. These triumphs were particularly special, as they marked the club's first major titles since its inception. The celebrations at the Red Bull Arena were undoubtedly electrifying, as the fans reveled in their team's success.

Beyond hosting RB Leipzig's home matches, the Red Bull Arena has also been a venue for other significant football events. In 2006, the stadium played host to several matches during the FIFA World Cup, including four first-round matches and one match in the round of 16. This showcased the Red Bull Arena's capability to host high-profile international tournaments.

The Red Bull Arena is not just a football stadium; it is a living room for RB Leipzig and its fans. It is a place where they gather to support their team, create lasting memories, and celebrate their successes. The stadium's imposing presence and modern facilities contribute to an unforgettable matchday experience for supporters.

Leipzig Stadium has been the home ground of RB Leipzig, a club playing in the Bundesliga which is the top division of German football. This stadium first opened its doors in 2004, but it was actually rebuilt within the shell of the old Zentralstadion stadium, which used to be the biggest stadium in former East Germany before reunification. One of the modern features of the current Leipzig Stadium is its state-of-the-art roof structure.

In 2024, Leipzig Stadium will have the honor of hosting several matches during the Euro 2024 tournament, which is the main championship for national teams in Europe organized by UEFA. The first match at this venue will take place on June 18th at 9pm, when Portugal takes on Czechia. Three days later on June 21st at 9pm, there will be another group stage game between

Netherlands and France playing at Leipzig Stadium.

The stadium will then host one more group stage match on June 24th at 9pm, with Croatia facing off against Italy. After the group stage, Leipzig Stadium is scheduled to hold a Round of 16 knockout match on July 2nd at 9pm between the teams that finish first in Group D and second in Group F. Hosting these Euro 2024 matches showcases Leipzig Stadium's capabilities to stage major international football tournaments.

2.8 Munich

Munich is a city located in southern Germany, the capital and largest city of the state of Bavaria. It has a population of around 1.5 million people within the city limits, making it the third-largest city in Germany after Berlin and Hamburg. Munich is situated about 50 km (31 miles) north of the Alps, at an altitude of about 520 meters (1,706 feet) above sea level. The local rivers are the Isar and the Würm.

Munich is a global center of science, technology, finance, innovation, business, and tourism. The city has a very high standard and quality of living, consistently ranking among the most livable cities in the world. Munich's economy is based on high-tech, automobiles, and the service sector, including IT, biotechnology, engineering, and electronics. It is home to many multinational companies such as BMW, Siemens, Allianz SE, and Munich Re. The city is also a significant financial center, second only to Frankfurt in Germany.

Historically, Munich has been a center of arts, architecture, culture, and science since the Renaissance and Baroque eras. The city was first mentioned in 1158, and it strongly resisted the Reformation, remaining a Catholic stronghold. After Bavaria became a kingdom in 1806, Munich became a major European center of arts and culture. During World War II, the city was heavily bombed, but it has restored most of its old town, boasting nearly 30,000 buildings from before the war.

Munich is known for its annual Oktoberfest, the world's largest Volksfest (beer festival and traveling funfair). The city's numerous architectural and cultural attractions, sports events, exhibitions, and the Oktoberfest attract considerable tourism. Munich's architecture includes notable buildings such as the

Frauenkirche (the city's cathedral), the Nymphenburg Palace, the Munich Residenz, and the Alte Pinakothek art museum.

The city has an extensive public transportation system consisting of an underground metro, trams, buses, and high-speed rail connections. Munich is a hub for regional transportation, with the second-largest airport in Germany and the Berlin–Munich high-speed railway connecting it to the German capital in about 4 hours.

Munich is subject to a long-term residential development plan aimed at addressing the acute housing crisis. The plan focuses on densifying existing housing estates, converting non-residential industrial areas into residential and mixed-use areas, and building new housing estates on greenfield sites in the city's periphery.

The city is home to several professional sports teams, including the famous football club FC Bayern Munich, which has won numerous national and international titles. Munich hosted the 1972 Summer Olympics, marred by the Munich massacre, and the 1974 FIFA World Cup final.

Munich has a beautiful cultural scene, with numerous museums, theaters, and festivals. The city is also a significant center for music, being the birthplace of prominent composers such as Richard Strauss and Carl Orff. Munich's nightlife is vibrant, with a high density of music venues, nightclubs, and bars.

In terms of geography, Munich lies on the elevated plains of Upper Bavaria, with a continental climate characterized by warm summers and cold winters. The city is surrounded by numerous freshwater lakes, such as Lake Starnberg, Ammersee, and Chiemsee, which are popular recreation destinations for residents.

Munich's population is diverse, with nearly 30% of residents being foreigners or German citizens with a migration background. The city has a long history of religious diversity, with significant Catholic, Protestant, and Muslim communities.

Munich is a vibrant, cosmopolitan city that serves as a major economic, cultural, and transportation hub in southern Germany. Its rich history, high standard of living, and numerous attractions make it a popular destination for tourists and a desirable place to live and work.

The Complete Fan's Companion to EURO 2024

2.8.1 **Allianz Arena**

The Allianz Arena is a massive football stadium located in Munich, Germany. It has a seating capacity of 75,000 for domestic matches and 70,000 for international and European matches. This makes it the second largest stadium in Germany, behind only the Westfalenstadion in Dortmund.

The stadium's unique design features thousands of inflated plastic air panels on the exterior facade that can be illuminated in different colors. Originally, the panels could only light up red for Bayern Munich matches, blue for 1860 Munich matches, and white for German national team matches. However, after an upgrade in 2015, the

LED lighting system can now display over 16 million different color combinations.

Construction on the Allianz Arena began in October 2002 after Munich voters approved building a new stadium at that location. It took two and a half years to complete, finally opening on May 30, 2005. The innovative design was created by the Swiss architecture firm Herzog & de Meuron. A key feature is the translucent exterior paneling that allows sunlight and air flow onto the playing surface to help the grass grow naturally.

When it first opened, the stadium was jointly owned by Bayern Munich and 1860 Munich, the two local professional football clubs. However, in 2006 Bayern purchased 1860's 50% ownership share for 11 million euros after 1860 faced bankruptcy. This allowed Bayern to be the sole tenant, although 1860 continued playing some home matches there until 2017 when Bayern terminated their rental agreement.

The large financial services company Allianz purchased 30-year naming rights to the stadium. However, due to sponsorship rules, the name "Allianz Arena" cannot be used for FIFA and UEFA matches. For those games it is referred to as the "FIFA World Cup Stadium Munich" or "Football Arena Munich" respectively.

The Allianz Arena has hosted many major football matches and tournaments over the years. It was one of the venues for the 2006 FIFA World Cup, hosting six matches including the semi-final between Portugal and France. It also hosted several UEFA Euro 2020 matches that were delayed until 2021 due to the COVID-19 pandemic, including a quarter-final match.

The Allianz Arena will host four group stage matches, one round of 16 match, and one semi-final at the upcoming UEFA Euro 2024 tournament.

The Allianz Arena is set to be a major venue for the UEFA Euro 2024 tournament hosted in Germany. It will kick things off by staging the opening match of the competition on June 14, 2024 when the German national team takes on Scotland at 9 PM local time in Group A action. The massive stadium will then host two more group stage matches on June 17th and June 20th, with Romania facing Ukraine at 3 PM in Group E and Slovenia taking on Serbia at 3 PM in Group C respectively. On June 25th, the Allianz Arena gets another group stage contest as Denmark battles Serbia at 9 PM in one of the final matches of that round. Once the knockout rounds begin, the arena will be the site of a Round of 16 match on July 2nd at 6 PM between the runner-up from Group E and one of the third-place teams from Groups A, B, C or D. Finally, the Allianz Arena will host one of the two semi-final matches on July 7th at 9 PM between the winners of the two quarterfinal ties played earlier that week, representing the last and biggest match to be staged at the iconic Munich stadium during the Euro 2024 tournament.

Other notable events it has hosted include the 2012 UEFA Champions League final where Chelsea upset Bayern Munich on penalties, and the first ever regular season NFL game played in

Germany in November 2022 between the Seattle Seahawks and Tampa Bay Buccaneers.

In addition to the playing area, the Allianz Arena features many amenities for fans. It has Europe's largest parking garage underneath with nearly 10,000 spaces. There are 28 food kiosks, restaurants and biergartens within the stadium itself. The FC Bayern Megastore covers 1000 square meters and sells every type of Bayern Munich merchandise imaginable.

After taking sole ownership in 2017, Bayern made some interior renovations to the Allianz Arena to give it more of their club identity. This included incorporating their team badge, club motto "Mia san mia" and red & white colors into the seating bowl and decor. Prior to that, the seating had been a neutral gray color.

The Allianz Arena is regarded as one of the great modern football stadiums in the world. Its exterior design, amenities, and ability to host major sporting events have made it a renowned venue for football in Germany and across Europe. As the home of hugely successful club Bayern Munich, it will undoubtedly continue hosting marquee matches and providing an outstanding experience for fans for many years to come.

2.9 Stuttgart

Stuttgart is a major industrial city located in southwest Germany. It is the capital and largest city of the state of Baden-Württemberg. With a population of around 630,000 people, Stuttgart is the sixth biggest city in Germany.

Stuttgart has a very strong economy and high standard of living. It consistently ranks among the wealthiest and most prosperous metropolitan areas in Europe. Major industries headquartered in Stuttgart include the famous automobile companies Mercedes-Benz and Porsche, as well as other giants like Bosch and Mahle. Because of this, Stuttgart is widely known as the "cradle of the automobile" and the birthplace of the car, which was first developed there by pioneers like Gottlieb Daimler and Karl Benz in the late 1800s.

Apart from the auto industry, Stuttgart is an important center for high-tech, engineering, electronics and financial services firms. It has the second largest stock exchange in Germany after Frankfurt. Over 11% of all research and development investment in Germany happens in the Stuttgart region. The area has a very high density of universities, research institutes, and scientific organizations.

Despite its very modern and high-tech economy, Stuttgart has a long history dating back thousands of years. It was first settled in ancient times and served as an important regional center under Roman rule. In the Middle Ages it grew into a prosperous trading town. Stuttgart's fortunes rose further when it became the capital of the state of Württemberg in the 1400s. It remained the capital of Württemberg until the end of the monarchy in 1918.

Today, Stuttgart features a mix of historic and modern architecture and landmarks. Some of the most notable older sites include the Old Castle, Collegiate Church, and various royal buildings and palaces from when it was the seat of the Württemberg kings and dukes. More recent architectural highlights are the Allianz Arena football stadium, Mercedes-Benz Museum, Porsche Museum, and the unique design of the Stuttgart Main Station.

Apart from its industrial and economic significance, Stuttgart also has a rich cultural life. It boasts high-quality museums, theaters, music venues and festivals. The Old State Gallery houses an impressive collection of European art from the 14th to 19th centuries. The Stuttgart Ballet company and State Opera are renowned internationally. The city hosts annual events like a huge Christmas market, spring festival, summer festival and wine village celebrations tied to its heritage of viniculture.

Stuttgart has a unique geographic setting, situated in a lush valley surrounded by hills, forests and vineyards. The valley location gave rise to its nickname as "The Stuttgart Cauldron." Despite being tucked in this bowl-shaped area, Stuttgart has excellent transportation links. It has a large international airport, high-speed rail connections to other major German cities, and a network of highways, rail lines and public transit to suburbs and surrounding towns.

Within the city itself, Stuttgart features many parks, gardens, cemeteries and green spaces. Some of the largest are the sprawling Schlossgarten, Rosensteinpark and the

Killesbergpark built on the grounds of a former stone quarry. The hilly terrain means there are over 400 public outdoor staircases and paths, known as the Stäffele, crisscrossing the city. These stairs between vineyards, gardens and neighborhoods are part of what gives Stuttgart a distinctive look and feel.

Stuttgart has hosted many major sporting events over the years, including matches for the 1974 and 2006 FIFA World Cup. It was also the site of the 1993 World Athletics Championships and has been home to prestigious tennis, cycling, gymnastics and other competitions. In addition to the Allianz Arena, other key sports venues are the Porsche Arena and facilities for hockey, swimming, boxing and more.

As for demographics, Stuttgart has an increasingly diverse population. Only around half of its residents have Swabian, or local German, roots. The city has welcomed many immigrants and foreign workers from Turkey, Greece, Italy, Croatia and other parts of southern Europe over the past decades. More recently, waves of refugees have arrived from conflicts in the Middle East and Africa.

In terms of religion, Stuttgart was historically a Protestant Christian city due to its status as part of the state of Württemberg during the Protestant Reformation. However, today only around one-quarter of the population is Protestant, while one-quarter is Catholic. The largest group, at nearly 50%, follows either no religion or faiths outside of Protestantism and Catholicism like Islam.

Stuttgart stands out as a center of industry, technology, prosperity and culture. From its automobile heritage to its modern economy, sporting events, parks and architecture, it is a unique German city with a lot to offer residents and visitors alike. Although often overshadowed by larger cities like Munich and Frankfurt, Stuttgart's role makes it vitally important within Germany and across Europe.

2.9.1 Stuttgart Arena Stadium

The Stuttgart Arena is a large multi-purpose stadium located in Stuttgart, Germany. It currently serves as the home venue for the Bundesliga football club VfB Stuttgart. Originally constructed between 1929-1933, the stadium has undergone several renovations and name changes over the decades.

The stadium first opened in 1933 under the name Stuttgarter Kampfbahn, but was then renamed the Adolf-Hitler-Kampfbahn during the Nazi era from 1933-1945. After World War II, it was temporarily called the Century Stadium from 1945-1949 before being renamed the Neckarstadion in 1949, a name it kept until 1993.

From 1993 to 2008, it was known as the Gottlieb-Daimler-Stadion, dedicated to the pioneer of the automotive industry Gottlieb Daimler. The stadium took on its current Mercedes-Benz Arena name in 2008 before a brand change in 2023 saw it renamed the MHP Arena.

The Complete Fan's Companion to EURO 2024

The MHP Arena has hosted many major sporting events over the years. It was one of the venues for the 1974 FIFA World Cup, hosting four matches during the tournament. It also staged two matches during the 1988 European Championship and six matches at the 2006 FIFA World Cup, including a Round of 16 game and the third-place playoff.

The stadium has also been the site for two European Cup/Champions League finals (1959 and 1988), the 1986 European Athletics Championships, the 1993 World Athletics Championships, and multiple American football Eurobowl finals in the 1990s.

The most recent major renovation occurred between 2009-2011 when the stadium was converted into a dedicated football arena. This involved demolishing the running track, lowering the pitch level, rebuilding the curved ends closer to the field, adding new seating sections, and extending the roof over the new areas.

Further upgrades were made from 2022-2024 in preparation for UEFA Euro 2024, including rebuilding the lower main stand, adding new team rooms, media facilities, and infrastructural improvements. The overall capacity is now 60,058 for domestic league matches and 54,812 for international matches due to some standing areas not being allowed under UEFA rules.

The MHP Arena follows a typical football stadium layout with four distinct stand sections. The Haupttribüne is the main stand along Mercedesstrasse housing VIP areas and press boxes. Opposite is the Gegentribüne stand formerly known by sponsor names.

Behind each goal is a curved end - the Cannstatter Kurve for VfB Stuttgart's ultras with terraced standing areas, and the Untertürkheimer Kurve containing away fan sections and additional hospitality areas.

A distinctive feature is the stadium's large sweeping fabric roof designed to resemble a saddle shape. Constructed in 1993, the PVC-coated polyester membrane roof is suspended from a heavy steel cable ring running around the entire stadium bowl.

Aside from sporting events, the stadium has historical significance as the place where Gottlieb Daimler tested some of the world's first motorcycles and automobiles with internal combustion engines in the 1880s on the nearby Mercedesstrasse.

The MHP Arena's location is part of the Neckarpark area next to other major venues like the Porsche Arena and Hanns-Martin-Schleyer-Halle. It is a short walk from the annual Cannstatter Volksfest, the Mercedes-Benz company headquarters and museum, and the VfB Stuttgart training grounds.

The MHP Arena will be one of the venues for the UEFA Euro 2024 tournament being co-hosted across Germany. It is scheduled to hold four group stage matches and one quarter-final match during the event:

June 16th, 2024 at 6pm: Slovenia vs Denmark

The Complete Fan's Companion to EURO 2024

June 19th, 2024 at 6pm: Germany vs Hungary

June 23rd, 2024 at 9pm: Scotland vs Hungary

June 26th, 2024 at 6pm: Ukraine vs Belgium

July 5th, 2024 at 6pm: Quarter-Final

The MHP Arena (formerly known by names like Neckarstadion and Gottlieb-Daimler-Stadion) is a large multipurpose stadium in Stuttgart that has hosted many major football matches and athletic events over the past 90 years. After extensive renovations, it will serve as one of the premier venues for the upcoming Euro 2024 tournament while continuing its primary role as the home ground of German club VfB Stuttgart.

The Complete Fan's Companion to EURO 2024

Chapter 3: History of the UEFA European Championship

The UEFA European Championship, also known as the Euros, is the primary association football tournament organized by the Union of European Football Associations (UEFA). It is a prestigious competition contested by the senior men's national teams of UEFA member nations to determine the continental champion of Europe.

The European Championship is the second-most watched football tournament in the world after the FIFA World Cup. The Euro 2016 final, for instance, attracted a global audience of around 600 million viewers. The tournament has been held every four years since 1960, with the exception of 2020, when it was postponed to

2021 due to the COVID-19 pandemic in Europe, although it retained the name Euro 2020.

Originally called the European Nations' Cup, the competition was renamed the UEFA European Championship in 1968. Since 1996, each individual event has been branded as "UEFA Euro"

Regional tournaments for national teams existed before the advent of a truly pan-European competition. The British Home Championship, which began in 1883, was an annual competition contested between the United Kingdom's four national teams: England, Scotland, Wales, and Ireland. Until these teams entered the FIFA World Cup in 1950, the Home Championship was the most important international tournament they participated in.

Similarly, from 1927 until 1960, the Central European International Cup brought together the national teams of Austria, Hungary, Italy, Czechoslovakia, Switzerland, and Yugoslavia.

The idea for a pan-European football tournament was first proposed by the French Football Federation's secretary-general Henri Delaunay in 1927. However, it wasn't until 1958, three years after Delaunay's death, that the tournament was officially launched. In honor of Delaunay, the trophy awarded to the champions is named after him.

The 1960 tournament, held in France, had four teams competing in the finals out of 17 that entered the qualification process. It was won by the Soviet Union, who defeated Yugoslavia 2–1 in a tense final in Paris. Notable absentees from the 17 teams that entered the qualifying tournament included England, the Netherlands, West Germany, and Italy.

Spain hosted the next tournament in 1964, which saw an increase in entries to 29 teams in the qualification tournament. West Germany was a notable absentee once again, and Greece withdrew after being drawn against Albania, with whom they were still at war. The hosts, Spain, beat the defending champions, the Soviet Union, 2-1 at the Santiago Bernabéu Stadium in Madrid.

The 1968 tournament, hosted and won by Italy, had the same tournament format as the previous editions. For the first and only time, a match was decided on a coin toss (the semi-final between Italy and the Soviet Union), and the final went to a replay after the match against Yugoslavia finished 1-1. Italy won the replay 2-0. More teams (31) entered this tournament, a testament to its growing popularity.

Belgium hosted the 1972 tournament, which West Germany won, beating the Soviet Union 3-0 in the final, with goals coming from Gerd Müller (twice) and Herbert Wimmer at the Heysel Stadium in Brussels. This tournament provided a preview of the West German team that would go on to win the 1974 FIFA World Cup.

The 1976 tournament in Yugoslavia was the last in which only four teams took part in the final tournament, and the last in which the hosts had to qualify. Czechoslovakia beat West Germany in the newly introduced penalty shootout. After seven successful conversions, Uli Hoeneß missed, leaving Czechoslovakian Antonín Panenka with the opportunity to score and win the tournament. An "audacious" chipped shot, described by UEFA as arguably the most renowned penalty kick in history, secured the victory as Czechoslovakia won 5-3 on penalties. The Panenka is a penalty kick technique where the player gently chips the ball rather than aiming for the sides of the goal. This subtle touch lifts the ball so it drops into the center of the net, tricking the goalkeeper, who usually dives to one side. This beautiful technique was used to score against West German goalkeeper Sepp Maier.

The competition was expanded to eight teams in the 1980 tournament, again hosted by Italy. It involved a group stage, with the winners of the groups going on to contest the final, and the runners-up playing in the third-place playoff.

The Complete Fan's Companion to EURO 2024

West Germany won their second European title by beating Belgium 2-1, with two goals scored by Horst Hrubesch at the Stadio Olimpico in Rome.

France won their first major title at home in the 1984 tournament, with their captain Michel Platini scoring 9 goals in just 5 games, including the opening goal in the final, in which they beat Spain 2-0. The format also changed, with the top two teams in each group going through to a semi-final stage instead of the winners of each group going straight into the final. The third-place playoff was also abolished.

West Germany hosted UEFA Euro 1988 but lost 2-1 to the Netherlands, their traditional rivals, in the semi-finals, which sparked vigorous celebrations in the Netherlands. The Netherlands went on to win the tournament in a rematch of their first game of the group stage, beating the Soviet Union 2-0 at the Olympia Stadion in Munich. Marco van Basten scored the second goal, a volley over the keeper from the right wing, which is often considered one of the best goals ever scored.

UEFA Euro 1992 was held in Sweden and was won by Denmark, who were only in the finals after UN sanctions prevented Yugoslavia's participation due to the ongoing conflicts in the region. The Danes beat holders the Netherlands on penalties in the semi-finals, then defeated world champion Germany 2-0. This was the first tournament in which a unified Germany took part and also the first major tournament to have the players' names printed on their backs.

England hosted UEFA Euro 1996, the first tournament to use the nomenclature "Euro 1996," and the number of teams taking part doubled to 16. The hosts were knocked out on penalties by Germany in a replay of the 1990 FIFA World Cup semi-final. The surprise team of the tournament was the newly formed Czech Republic, participating in its first international competition following the dissolution of Czechoslovakia. They reached the final after beating Portugal and France in the knockout stage. Germany would go on to win the final 2–1 thanks to the first golden goal ever in a major tournament, scored by Oliver Bierhoff five minutes into extra time. This was Germany's first title as a unified nation.

UEFA Euro 2000 was the first tournament to be held by two countries, the Netherlands and Belgium. France, the reigning World Cup champions, were favored to win, and they lived up to expectations when they beat Italy 2–1 after extra time, having come from being 1–0 down. Sylvain Wiltord equalized in the last minute of regular time, and David Trezeguet scored the winning golden goal in extra time.

UEFA Euro 2004 produced an upset: Greece, who had only qualified for one World Cup (1994) and one European Championship (1980) before, beat hosts Portugal 1–0 in the final with a goal scored by Angelos Charisteas in the 57th minute to win a tournament that they had been given odds of 150–1 to win before it began. On their way to the final, they also beat holders France as well as the Czech Republic.

The 2008 tournament, hosted by Austria and Switzerland, marked the second time that two nations co-hosted and the first edition where the new trophy was awarded. The final between Germany and Spain was held at the Ernst Happel Stadion in Vienna. Spain defeated Germany 1-0, with a goal scored by Fernando Torres in the 33rd minute, sparking much celebration across the country. This was their first title since the 1964 tournament.

Spain became the first nation to defend a European Championship title at UEFA Euro 2012, co-hosted by Poland and Ukraine. They defeated Italy 4-0 in the final, thus becoming the first European team to win three consecutive major tournaments. In scoring the third goal of the final, Torres became the first player to score in two European Championship finals.

The Complete Fan's Companion to EURO 2024

In 2007, UEFA announced plans to expand the tournament from 16 to 24 teams, starting from 2016. Euro 2016, hosted by France, was the first to feature 24 teams in the finals. Portugal, which qualified for the knockout phase despite finishing third in its group, went on to win the championship by defeating the heavily favored host team France 1-0 in the final, thanks to a goal from Eder in the 109th minute. This was the first time Portugal won a major tournament.

For the 2020 tournament, originally scheduled for 2020 but postponed to 2021 due to the COVID-19 pandemic, UEFA announced that the tournament would be hosted in several cities across Europe, with the semi-finals and final being played in London. In the final, Italy defeated first-time finalists England 3-2 on penalties after the game was tied 1-1 after extra time, to win their second European Championship.

The Trophy

The trophy awarded to the winner of the European Championship is named after the Henri Delaunay.

The trophy awarded to the winner of the European Championship is named the Henri Delaunay Trophy, in honor of Henri Delaunay, the first General Secretary of UEFA who came up with the idea of a European championship but died five years before the first tournament in 1960.

The original trophy bore the words "Coupe d'Europe" (European Cup), "Coupe Henri

Delaunay" (Henri Delaunay Cup), and "Championnat d'Europe" (European Championship) on the front and had a juggling boy on the back. The winners were allowed to keep the trophy for four years until the next tournament.

For the 2008 tournament, the Henri Delaunay Trophy was remodeled to make it larger, as the old one was overshadowed by UEFA's other trophies. The new trophy, made of sterling silver, weighs 8 kilograms and is 60 centimeters tall. The marble plinth was removed and the names of the winning countries are now engraved on the back under the words "Coupe Henri Delaunay" in English rather than French. The juggling boy was also returned on the trophy's back in 2016.

How Team Qualify

To qualify for the European Championship finals, all UEFA member nations except the designated host(s) go through a qualifying process. The format has varied over the years, but generally involves teams being drawn into groups and playing home-and-away matches on a league basis, with the leading teams in each group qualifying directly for the finals.

In recent tournaments, some remaining places have been decided through play-off matches. The qualifying phase begins in the autumn after the preceding FIFA World Cup, almost two years before the finals tournament itself.

Initially, the host nation for the finals was selected from the four teams that qualified. But since the expansion to eight finalists in 1980, the host(s) automatically qualify, along with the leading teams from the qualifying groups.

Participating Teams

A total of 55 national teams currently compete in European Championship qualifying, representing all the current UEFA member associations. Some nations like England, Scotland, Wales and Northern Ireland competed as part of other team setups like the United Kingdom (British Home Championship) or Yugoslavia before becoming independent entries.

East Germany was a participating team until reunification with West Germany in 1990 to form the present-day Germany team. Similarly, Russia took over the spot of the Soviet Union after its dissolution, while Czech Republic and Slovakia emerged as successors to Czechoslovakia.

New nations formed from the break-up of Yugoslavia like Croatia, Slovenia, Bosnia & Herzegovina, Serbia, Montenegro, North Macedonia and Kosovo have appeared as separate teams since the mid-1990s.

As of 2021, a total of 10 national teams have been crowned European champions over the 16 tournaments held so far.

Germany (including former West Germany) and Spain have had the most success, winning three titles each. Italy and France have won two titles apiece, while the Soviet Union, Czechoslovakia, Netherlands, Denmark, Greece and Portugal have won one title each.

Spain became the first team to win consecutive titles in 2008 and 2012. Germany and Spain's three titles make them the most successful nations in the competition's history.

Some notable teams that have reached the final without winning include England (runners-up in 2020), Belgium (runners-up in 1980) and the former Yugoslavia (runners-up in 1960 and 1968).

3.1 Records and Statistics

There are several individual and team records associated with the European Championship Finals:

The Complete Fan's Companion to EURO 2024

- Michel Platini of France holds the record for most goals scored in a single tournament final with 9 goals in 1984.

- Cristiano Ronaldo has scored the most total goals across all European Championship final tournaments with 14 goals.

- Spain's Fernando Torres is the only player to have scored in two European Championship finals (2008 and 2012).

- The highest scoring final was Portugal's 4-0 win over Germany in the 2000 tournament.

- The Netherlands 6-1 victory over Yugoslavia in 2000 is the highest scoring match in tournament finals history.

- Germany has appeared in the most finals (6 times) while Spain and Germany have won the most titles (3 each).

Team Debuts and Appearances

One of the most intriguing aspects of the Euros is the participation and debut of national teams throughout its history. Germany, formerly known as West Germany, holds the record for the most appearances, having participated in an impressive 13 tournaments since their debut in 1972. Closely following are Russia, formerly the Soviet Union, with 12 appearances, and Spain with 11 appearances.

The 1960 edition of the Euros saw the debut of four teams: Czechoslovakia, France, the Soviet Union, and Yugoslavia. With each subsequent tournament, new nations have joined the fray, adding to the diversity and excitement of the event. The 2016 edition witnessed the highest number of debutants, with five teams – Albania, Iceland, Northern Ireland, Wales, and Slovakia – making their first appearances.

General Team Records

The Euros have been a stage for nations to etch their names in the annals of history through their outstanding performances. Based on a points system that awards three points for a win, one for a draw, and none for a loss, Germany leads the overall team records with an impressive 94 points, followed closely by Italy with 81 points and Spain with 78 points.

Germany's dominance is further exemplified by their 27 wins, the highest in the tournament's history. Interestingly, Denmark holds the unenviable record of the most losses with 17, while Italy has the most draws with 18.

In terms of goal-scoring prowess, Germany once again tops the charts with a staggering 78 goals scored, closely followed by France with 69 goals and Spain with 68 goals. However, it is the Netherlands that boasts the highest average of goals scored per match, with an impressive 1.67 goals per game.

Medals

West Germany/Germany leads the pack with an astonishing nine medals, including three gold, three silver, and three bronze. Spain and Italy follow closely with five medals each, while France has secured four medals.

Looking at the final results, Like I pointed out above, West Germany/Germany and Spain share the record for the most championship titles, with three each. Italy and France are not far behind, with two titles apiece. Interestingly, the Soviet Union, now Russia, has won the tournament once but has finished as runners-up on three occasions, the joint-most alongside West Germany/Germany.

Let's look at the tournament progression and streaks. The Euros have witnessed remarkable streaks and progressions throughout their history. Portugal holds the record for the most consecutive progressions from the group stage, achieving this feat an impressive eight times between 1984 and 2020. In contrast, Scotland has the unfortunate distinction of being the team with the most appearances without ever progressing from the group stage, with three such instances.

When it comes to winning streaks, several teams have etched their names in the record books. France, the Netherlands, the Czech Republic, and Italy have all recorded five consecutive wins in the tournament, while Italy holds the remarkable record for the most consecutive wins across both qualifying and final tournaments, with an incredible 15 victories between March 2019 and July 2021.

Awards

UEFA instituted official awards starting from the 1996 tournament. These include:

- Player of the Tournament award for the best player
- Top Scorer award for the most prolific goalscorer
- Young Player of the Tournament award for the best U-21 player (from 2016)
- Man of the Match award for standout performances in each game
- Team of the Tournament award for the best combined team

Not to forget the individual brilliance

The Euros have been a stage for individual brilliance, with several players leaving an indelible mark on the tournament's history.

The Complete Fan's Companion to EURO 2024

Cristiano Ronaldo, the Portuguese talisman, holds the record for the most goals scored in final tournaments with an astonishing 14 goals, as well as the most appearances in the tournament with 25.

In terms of single-tournament goalscoring exploits, Michel Platini's incredible tally of nine goals for France in the 1984 edition remains unmatched. Platini also holds the record for the fastest hat-trick in the Euros, achieved in a blistering 18 minutes against Yugoslavia in the same tournament.

A total of 322 players have been part of the winning team in the tournament's history. Among them, only 13 players have won the title twice, with Rainer Bonhof being the sole non-Spanish player to achieve this feat.

Cristiano Ronaldo holds the record for the most appearances in the European Championship finals, having participated in five tournaments (2004, 2008, 2012, 2016, and 2020). Iker Casillas and Gianluigi Buffon follow closely, with five and four appearances, respectively.

In terms of most matches played, Cristiano Ronaldo leads the pack with 25 appearances, followed by João Moutinho and Pepe, both with 19 matches each. Leonardo Bonucci, Bastian Schweinsteiger, Gianluigi Buffon, Giorgio Chiellini, Jordi Alba, Cesc Fàbregas, Andrés Iniesta, Rui Patrício, Lilian Thuram, and Edwin van der Sar have all played more than 15 matches in the European Championship.

Goalkeeping Exploits

Goalkeepers have played a crucial role in shaping the fortunes of teams in the Euros, and their contributions have not gone unnoticed. Edwin van der Sar of the Netherlands and Iker Casillas of Spain share the record for the most clean sheets (matches without conceding a goal) in the tournament, with an impressive nine each.

In a single tournament, Iker Casillas and Jordan Pickford of England hold the record for the most clean sheets, with five apiece, in the 2012 and 2020 editions, respectively. Casillas also holds the record for the most consecutive minutes without conceding a goal in the finals, with an impressive 519 minutes.

Coaching Prowess

Behind every successful team lies the guiding hand of a skilled coach. The role of the manager in this tournament is crucial, as they are responsible for selecting the squad, developing tactics, and leading the team to victory. Winning the European Championship is a significant achievement, and the pressure on the managers is immense due to the limited contact they have with the players during the regular club season.

The first manager to win the UEFA European Championship was Gavriil Kachalin, who guided the Soviet Union to victory in the inaugural tournament in 1960. It is noteworthy that no manager has won the title on more than one occasion, and all winning managers have won it with their native countries, except for the German coach Otto Rehhagel, who led Greece to triumph in 2004.

While no coach has won the Euros more than once, several have left an indelible mark on the tournament. Joachim Löw of Germany holds the record for the most matches coached (21) and the most matches won (12) in the Euros.

Lars Lagerbäck and Joachim Löw share the distinction of being involved in the most tournaments, with four each. Interestingly, several coaches, including Guus Hiddink, Giovanni Trapattoni, Dick Advocaat, Lars Lagerbäck, and Fernando Santos, have had the unique experience of coaching two different nations in the Euros.

Two managers have experienced the joy of winning and the agony of losing a European Championship final: Helmut Schön (winner in

1972 and runner-up in 1976, both with West Germany) and Berti Vogts (winner in 1996 and runner-up in 1992, both with Germany). Remarkably, Vogts is the only person to have won the European Championship as both a player and a manager, having previously lifted the trophy while playing for West Germany in 1972.

Schön and Vicente del Bosque hold the unique distinction of being the only managers to have won both the European Championship and the FIFA World Cup. Schön guided Germany to the 1974 World Cup after winning the European Championship in 1972.

José Villalonga holds the record for being the youngest manager to win the European Championship. He was 44 years and 192 days old when he led Spain to victory in 1964. On the other hand, Luis Aragonés is the oldest manager to have won the tournament, having guided Spain to triumph in 2008 at the age of 69 years and 336 days.

Discipline and Controversies

The Euros have not been without their fair share of controversies and disciplinary incidents. Radoslav Látal of the Czech Republic holds the unfortunate record of being the player with the most sendings-off (red cards) in the tournament's history, with two dismissals.

The 2000 edition witnessed the highest number of sendings-off in a single tournament, with 10 players being shown the red card across 31 matches. The Netherlands holds the team record for the most sendings-off overall, with four dismissals.

In terms of cautions (yellow cards), Giorgos Karagounis of Greece tops the list with eight cautions across his appearances in the tournament. The 2016 edition saw a staggering 205 cautions issued, the highest in a single tournament.

Attendance and Atmosphere

The Euros have always been a spectacle that captivates audiences worldwide, and the attendance figures reflect the passion and fervor surrounding the tournament. The highest attendance for a single match was recorded in the 1964 final between the Soviet Union and

Spain, with a staggering 79,115 spectators packing the iconic Santiago Bernabéu Stadium in Madrid.

While the 1960 edition witnessed the lowest total attendance of 78,958, the 2016 tournament set a new record with an impressive 2,427,303 total attendance. The 1988 edition holds the distinction of the highest average attendance per match, with 59,243 spectators on average.

Penalty Shoot-outs and Drama

The Euros have witnessed numerous nail-biting penalty shoot-outs, adding to the drama and excitement of the tournament. Italy holds the record for the most shoot-outs participated in, with seven, closely followed by Spain with four.

The 1996 and 2020 editions saw the highest number of shoot-outs in a single tournament, with four each. Italy and Spain share the record for the most shoot-out wins, with four each, while England holds the unfortunate distinction of the most shoot-out losses, with four.

In terms of individual performances during shoot-outs, several players have etched their names in the record books. Zinedine Zidane, Youri Djorkaeff, Bixente Lizarazu, Vincent Guérin, and Laurent Blanc of France, as well as Cristiano Ronaldo of Portugal, have all successfully converted two penalties each in shoot-outs.

Gianluigi Donnarumma of Italy and Unai Simón of Spain share the record for the most saves in a single tournament, with three each, while

The Complete Fan's Companion to EURO 2024

Gianluigi Buffon of Italy holds the overall record for the most successful kicks in shoot-outs, with an impressive 29 out of 41 attempts.

The UEFA European Championship has been a showcase of the highest level of soccer talent, passion, and drama. From the early days of the tournament to the present, records have been set, broken, and etched into the annals of history. As we look forward to this edition of the Euro and many more, we can anticipate more thrilling moments, remarkable achievements, and the creation of new records that will further cement the tournament's legacy as one of the most prestigious and captivating international soccer events.

Chapter 4: Groups and Teams

The groups have been drawn as follows: **Group A** consists of Germany (the host nation), Scotland, Hungary, and Switzerland. **Group B** includes Spain, Croatia, Italy, and Albania. England, Denmark, Serbia, and Slovenia make up **Group C**. The strong **Group D** comprises France, Netherlands, Austria, and Poland. In Group E, we have Belgium, Slovakia, Romania, and Ukraine. Group F features Portugal, Czechia, Turkey, and Georgia.

The tournament will begin with a group stage where each team plays three games against the other teams in their group. The top two teams from each of the eight groups will automatically advance to the knockout rounds.

The Complete Fan's Companion to EURO 2024

If two or more teams have the same number of points after all their group games, there are several rules to determine which team finishes higher in the group.

First, they look at just the games between the tied teams. The team with more points from those head-to-head games finishes higher. If still tied, they use goal difference from the head-to-head games as the next tiebreaker, followed by total goals scored in those games.

If teams are still level after applying those first three criteria to just their head-to-head results, those same three criteria are rechecked using all group games.

After that, the next tiebreakers are: overall goal difference from all games, total goals scored in

The Complete Fan's Companion to EURO 2024

all games, disciplinary record (fewer yellow/red cards), and finally the team's qualifying ranking if they cannot be separated.

There is also a special rule - if two specific teams are tied on everything after the final group games, their ranking is decided by a penalty shootout between just those two teams.

The rules go through several stages to try to definitively separate any teams that finished with the same number of group points.

Additionally, four of the third-placed teams across all groups with the best records will also qualify for the next stage.

The group stage matches are scheduled to commence on June 14th, 2024. Once the group stage concludes, the knockout phase will kick off on June 30th with the Round of 16. The competition will then progress through the quarter-finals and semi-finals before reaching the grand finale.

The Euro 2024 final will take place on July 14th, 2024, in the German capital city of Berlin. This highly anticipated match will determine the new European champions, who will be crowned with continental glory for the next four years.

An important regulation for this tournament is that each team's squad can consist of a maximum of 26 players and a minimum of 23 players. Furthermore, it is mandatory for every team to include at least three goalkeepers in their final squad, as per FIFA rules introduced in 1934.

The Complete Fan's Companion to EURO 2024

Chapter 5: Group Stage Draw Analysis

Group A of the upcoming Euro 2024 tournament is shaping up to be an absolute cracker. As the host nation, all eyes will be on Germany to see if they can recapture the glory days of their three European Championship triumphs in 1972, 1980 and 1996. However, Julian Nagelsmann's side won't have it all their own way in a group that contains some potentially tricky opposition.

The Germans currently sit 16th in the latest FIFA world rankings, making them the highest ranked team in the group on paper. Their star-studded squad blends experience and youth, with venerable campaigners like Thomas Muller, Toni Kroos and Ilkay Gundogan complemented by some of the brightest young talents in European football right now. Players like Jamal Musiala, Florian Wirtz and Kai Havertz could well be the stars to watch.

As hosts, Germany avoided qualifying, but their preparations haven't been completely smooth sailing under Nagelsmann's tenure so far. A run of slightly underwhelming results, including a shock defeat to Hungary in the Nations League in 2022, has taken a bit of the sheen off their trophy credentials. Make no mistake though, on home soil and with a partisan crowd behind them, Germany will be desperate to hit the ground running and stamp their authority on Group A.

Their opening test is a potential banana skin against familiar foes Scotland on June 14th in Munich. Despite holding a convincing head-to-head advantage over the years, Germany's recent meetings with Scotland have been much tighter affairs. The two sides traded home wins in Euro 2016 qualifying, with Thomas Muller netting a brace in each victory. Those results suggest the plucky Scots, while underdogs, shouldn't be taken lightly by Nagelsmann's troops.

Scotland's very presence at Euro 2024 is an achievement in itself, with this being their first major tournament appearance since the 1998 World Cup in France. Steve Clarke has masterminded an impressive qualification campaign that has the Tartan Army believing they can make an impact. In Andrew Robertson, John McGinn and Kieran Tierney, they possess players with the experience and quality to cause an upset on their day.

The Scots also have an exciting crop of emerging talents like Billy Gilmour and Nathan Patterson providing bite and energy to complement the more battle-hardened professionals in the ranks. While Scotland's current FIFA ranking of 39th makes them the lowest ranked team in Group A, they will relish the opportunity to show they belong among the European elite.

For Scotland, navigating their way past the other teams in Group A may represent their most realistic path to the knockout rounds. Their head-to-head record against Germany suggests an upset on opening night is not completely out of the question. But perhaps more realistically, they'll be targeting maximum points from their fixtures against Hungary and Switzerland.

Hungary, for their part, have become a regular feature at European Championship finals in recent years, with Euro 2024 representing their third consecutive tournament appearance at this level. However, unlike their previous qualifications which were achieved through play-offs, this time the Hungarians topped their group to seal progress to Germany - a first for them since way back in 1986.

Under the astute guidance of Italian manager Marco Rossi, the current Hungarian crop look a well-balanced blend of youth and experience capable of springing a surprise or two. Experienced heads like goalkeeper Peter Gulacsi and striker Adam Szalai provide the backbone, but it's the emerging talents like RB Leipzig's Dominik Szoboszlai and Freiburg's Roland Sallai who carry Hungary's biggest threat.

The Complete Fan's Companion to EURO 2024

The Hungarians currently sit 26th in the FIFA world rankings, making them the second highest ranked team in Group A after Germany. Their recent head-to-head record against *Die Mannschaft* is also incredibly encouraging from a Hungarian perspective. As well as earning a 1-1 draw in the Nations League in 2022, Hungary actually beat Germany 1-0 in the same competition in 2022 - their first win over the European giants in 18 years.

Those recent results against Germany, combined with Hungary's eye-catching Euro 2024 qualification campaign where they topped a group containing Serbia, suggest Rossi's side will fancy their chances of progressing from Group A. Their tournament kicks off with a potentially crucial clash against Switzerland on June 15th in Cologne.

The Swiss themselves boast a relatively strong pedigree at European Championship finals, having qualified for their fifth tournament in the last seven editions. Currently ranked 19th in the world by FIFA, Murat Yakin's well-organized team could prove to be a dark horse in Germany this summer.

Like several teams in the group, Switzerland's squad has a lovely blend of youth and experience about it. In Granit Xhaka and Xherdan Shaqiri they possess two of the most consistent and talented midfield operators in European football over the past decade. The menacing presence of Monaco striker Breel Embolo leads the Swiss attack, while experienced heads like Yann

The Complete Fan's Companion to EURO 2024

Sommer and Ricardo Rodriguez marshal the defense.

However, the Swiss do have a couple of potential stumbling blocks on the horizon based on their recent head-to-head record with Group A opponents. Their 5-2 thumping at the hands of Hungary in 2017 will no doubt have been noted by Rossi's side ahead of their opening fixture in Cologne. Shutting down the Swiss midfield runners and supply lines to Embolo will be key for Hungary.

Scotland's head-to-head record against Switzerland is abysmal. In the UEFA Futsal Euro qualification match between Switzerland and Scotland on April 11, 2024, Switzerland won 3-1. Earlier, on February 1, 2019, during the World Cup qualifying, Scotland played against

Switzerland and lost 1-4. Another encounter between the two teams took place on January 24, 2017, where Switzerland defeated Scotland 6-2.There's every chance their Group A clash on June 19th in Cologne could be a closely-fought, cagey affair settled by a moment of magic or a decisive set-piece intervention from one of Xhaka, McGinn or Shaqiri.

When the group stage draw was initially made, this Group A was identified by many as potentially being one of the closest, most competitive sections to call. And all the evidence surrounding the historical head-to-head records, recent form, and blending of youth and experience in the respective squads suggests that prediction could well be accurate.

Of course, on paper at least, Germany go into their home Euro 2024 tournament as the favourites to top Group A and seal safe progress to the knockout rounds. Their status as hosts, strong recent tournament pedigree, and the sheer weight of attacking talent in Nagelsmann's squad marks them out as the team to beat.

However, their recent struggles against Hungary in 2021/2022 and the threat of potential banana skins against spirited opponents like Scotland and Switzerland mean Germany cannot simply turn up and expect to swat teams aside. The group phase presents multiple potential pitfalls that Nagelsmann and his players must skillfully navigate.

For Hungary, their current stable of players and tactics under the shrewd Rossi bode well for a potential run to the knockouts. Their opening fixture against the Swiss could be pivotal in deciding who finishes Group A runners-up behind the likely group winners Germany. The head-to-head history suggests there's little to split the two sides.

From a Scottish perspective, Steven Clarke's side may need to draw inspiration from past underdog tales to progress from this group. But in players like Robertson, McGinn and the emerging Gilmour, they possess the quality to potentially cause an upset or two. Taking four points from their triple-header against Hungary and Switzerland is likely the minimum needed to have a chance of squeaking through.

Switzerland, for all their strength and consistent tournament pedigree, are not dead certs to make the knockouts themselves from Group A. Their head-to-heads with Hungary and Scotland suggest both of those sides can pose a real threat to their qualification ambitions if Xhaka, Embolo and co. are not fully focused.

Looking at the group overall, it's refreshingly difficult to say with any real conviction who the two qualifiers will ultimately be come the end of the round-robin phase. That owes a lot to the respective levels of quality, experience and potential match-winners scattered throughout all four squads. From the veteran guile of Muller and Gundogan to the youthful explosiveness of Musiala, Wirtz and Szoboszlai, Group A is not short of potential grand performers ready to light up Euro 2024.

When the circus rolls into Munich for the opening fixtures on June 14th, all four nations in this group can realistically stake a claim for being contenders to progress to the knockout rounds. But, of course, soccer is a funny old game, as the cliché goes. One momentary lapse, a singular stroke of genius, a harsh referee decision - the thinnest of margins could be all it takes to completely alter the prevailing narratives.

5.1 Group B Analysis

The Group of Death is upon us, and it promises to be an exhilarating affair. With three teams ranked in FIFA's Top 10 – Spain, Croatia, and Italy – this group is a true test of mettle, where only the strongest will emerge victorious. The battle lines have been drawn, and the stage is set for an epic showdown.

Spain, the reigning champions of the UEFA Nations League, enter the fray with a formidable squad led by the experienced Luis de la Fuente. Having orchestrated a remarkable turnaround for *La Roja*, de la Fuente's tactical acumen and man-management skills will be put to the ultimate test. Boasting a star-studded lineup featuring the likes of Álvaro Morata, Dani Olmo, and the ever-reliable Rodri, Spain's possession-based style promises to be a treat for the neutral spectator.

However, their path to glory will not be an easy one, as they face a familiar foe in Croatia. The Vatreni, led by the legendary Zlatko Dalić, have established themselves as a force to be reckoned with on the international stage. With stalwarts like Luka Modrić and Marcelo Brozović pulling the strings in midfield, and the lethal Andrej Kramarić leading the line, Croatia's tactical versatility and never-say-die attitude make them a daunting opponent for any team.

The addition of Italy to this group only adds to the intrigue. The Azzurri, under the guidance of the charismatic Luciano Spalletti, have undergone a renaissance of sorts. With a squad brimming with talent, including the likes of Federico Chiesa, Nicolò Barella, and the evergreen Gianluigi Donnarumma, Italy's brand of attacking football promises to be a spectacle. Their recent friendly victories against Ecuador and Venezuela only serve as a reminder of their prowess on the big stage.

Amidst this heavyweight clash, the dark horse of the group emerges in the form of Albania. Led by the Brazilian tactician Sylvinho, the Eagles have defied all odds to secure their place in the European Championship. With an experienced core of players like Elseid Hysaj, Berat Gjimshiti, and Sokol Cikalleshi, Albania's never-say-die attitude could prove to be a stumbling block for their more illustrious opponents.

As we go deeper into this tantalizing group, the head-to-head factor becomes a crucial element to consider. Spain and Italy have a long-standing rivalry, often referred to as the "Mediterranean Derby." Their recent encounters have been closely contested affairs, with Spain emerging victorious in the UEFA Nations League final in 2023, while Italy exacted revenge in the European Championship final just two years prior. The upcoming matches between these two heavyweights promise to be nothing short of epic.

Croatia, too, has a storied history with Spain, with their most recent clash ending in a narrow 1-0 victory for *La Roja* in the UEFA Nations League. However, the Vatreni's never-say-die attitude and their ability to rise to the occasion in major tournaments cannot be overlooked. Their head-to-head encounters with Italy, while less frequent, have been equally enthralling, with both teams boasting rich footballing pedigrees.

Albania, the underdogs of the group, have their work cut out for them. While they may lack the star power of their opponents, their recent draw against Moldova and a hard-fought victory over Bulgaria in the European qualifiers serve as a proof of their resilience. Their encounters with Italy, though historically one-sided, offer a glimmer of hope, as they seek to etch their names in the annals of European football history.

As we look ahead to the upcoming matches, the air is thick with anticipation and uncertainty. Each team boasts a wealth of talent and tactics, making predictions a perilous exercise. However, one thing is certain – this Group of Death promises to be a spectacle like no other, where the line between triumph and heartbreak is razor-thin.

In this crucible of footballing excellence, the slightest misstep could prove fatal. The pressure will be immense, and the stakes have never been higher. For Spain, Croatia, and Italy, this group represents an opportunity to cement their legacy as giants of the game. For Albania, it is a chance to defy the odds and etch their names in footballing folklore.

Buckle up, football fans, for this promises to be a rollercoaster ride of emotions, where dreams will be realized and hearts will be broken. In the end, only the strongest will prevail.

5.2 **Group C Analysis**

At the forefront of this heavyweight clash stand two heavyweights: England and Denmark. Both nations have tasted the sweet nectar of European Championship triumph, with the Three Lions emerging as runners-up in the historic Euro 2020, while the Danish Dynamite etched their names in folklore by claiming the coveted crown in 1992. These two giants of the game are no strangers to the grandest of stages, and their impending showdown promises to be a battle for the ages.

Leading the English charge is Gareth Southgate, a man whose tactical acumen and man-management skills have earned him a place among the most respected coaches in the modern era. With a squad brimming with talent, including the prolific Harry Kane, the dynamic Real Madrid star, Jude Bellingham, and Arsenal's Saka, England will undoubtedly be a force to be reckoned with. Southgate's pragmatic approach and ability to adapt to any situation make the Three Lions a formidable opponent, capable of dismantling even the most resolute defenses.

On the other hand, Denmark's hopes rest on the shoulders of Kasper Hjulmand, a mastermind whose tactical prowess has propelled the Danish team to new heights. With a squad that boasts the likes of Christian Eriksen, the evergreen midfield maestro, and the rising star Rasmus Højlund, Denmark's attacking prowess is sure to strike fear into the hearts of their opponents. Hjulmand's ability to mold his team into a cohesive unit, coupled with their never-say-die attitude, makes the Danes a force to be reckoned with.

But this group is far from a two-horse race. Lurking in the shadows are Serbia and Slovenia, two nations with a rich footballing heritage and a burning desire to make their mark on the European stage.

Serbia, led by the charismatic Dragan Stojković, has emerged as a dark horse in recent years.

The Complete Fan's Companion to EURO 2024

With a squad spearheaded by the indomitable Aleksandar Mitrović and the midfield dynamo Sergej Milinković-Savić, the Eagles have the potential to soar above expectations. Stojković's tactical nous and motivational prowess have galvanized this Serbian side, transforming them into a formidable opponent capable of upending even the most illustrious of foes.

Meanwhile, Slovenia, under the guidance of the experienced Matjaž Kek, will be seeking to make their mark on the European stage. With a squad that boasts the talents of Jan Oblak, one of the finest goalkeepers of his generation, and the emerging starlet Benjamin Šeško, Slovenia has the potential to be a thorn in the side of their more illustrious opponents. Kek's pragmatic approach and his team's resilience make them a force to be reckoned with, capable of springing surprises on the grandest of stages.

Their most recent clash, a friendly on March 26, 2024, ended in a 2-2 stalemate. However, England will undoubtedly be seeking redemption for their 0-2 defeat at the hands of Denmark in the UEFA Nations League back in November 2023.

The encounters between England and Serbia, on the other hand, have been few and far between, but no less intense. Their most recent meeting, a 1-1 draw on November 20, 2023, in the European qualifiers, was a hard-fought affair that left both teams with a point to prove. As for England's clashes with Slovenia, the Three Lions have traditionally held the upper hand, with their most recent encounter, a 1-0 victory on October 5, 2017, serving as a reminder of their dominance.

Denmark's encounters with Serbia have been equally enthralling, with the Danes emerging victorious in their most recent clash, a 3-0 triumph on March 29, 2022. However, the Eagles will undoubtedly be seeking to avenge that defeat and assert their dominance on the European stage. As for Denmark's clashes with Slovenia, the two nations have a rich history, with their most recent encounter, a 2-1 victory for Denmark on November 17, 2023, in the European qualifiers, adding another chapter to their storied rivalry.

For England, the road to redemption begins here. Having tasted the bitter sting of defeat in the Euro 2020 final, the Three Lions will be driven by a burning desire to make amends. With Kane leading the charge and Southgate's tactical nous guiding them, England will undoubtedly be a force to be reckoned with. However, they will face stiff competition from their illustrious rivals, each of whom possesses the talent and determination to thwart England's quest for glory.

Denmark, too, will be seeking to cement their place among the European elite. With Eriksen pulling the strings and Højlund leading the line, the Danes possess the firepower to dismantle even the most resolute defenses. Hjulmand's tactical flexibility and his team's unwavering spirit make them a formidable opponent, one that will undoubtedly relish the opportunity to showcase their talents on the grandest of stages.

The Complete Fan's Companion to EURO 2024

Serbia, the dark horse of the group, will be seeking to defy the odds and silence their doubters. With Mitrović spearheading the attack and Milinković-Savić orchestrating the midfield, the Eagles possess the talent to soar above expectations. Stojković's tactical nous and motivational prowess have galvanized this Serbian side, instilling in them a belief that they can conquer any obstacle that stands in their path.

And then there is Slovenia, the underdogs of the group, but by no means pushovers. With Oblak marshaling the defense and Šeško leading the line, Slovenia possesses the talent to spring surprises on the grandest of stages. Kek's pragmatic approach and his team's resilience make them a force to be reckoned with.

In the end, only two teams will emerge from this team.

5.3 Group D Analysis

With powerhouses like France, the Netherlands, Austria, and Poland vying for the top two spots that would secure their advancement to the knockout stage, this Group D promises to be fierce and unpredictable.

Let's start by examining the teams and their respective strengths and weaknesses.

France: *Les Bleus*
Ranked second in the world according to the latest FIFA rankings, France is undoubtedly one of the favorites to lift the trophy. Led by the

experienced Didier Deschamps, who guided them to their second European Championship triumph in 2000, Les Bleus boast a formidable squad brimming with talent.

Kylian Mbappé, the captain and talisman of the team, is widely regarded as one of the best players in the world. His blistering pace, clinical finishing, and overall brilliance on the pitch make him a constant threat to any defense. Alongside him, the likes of Antoine Griezmann, Olivier Giroud, and Ousmane Dembélé form a potent attacking force that can overwhelm even the most resolute defenses.

However, France's defensive prowess should not be overlooked. With players like Raphael Varane, Presnel Kimpembe. Although Hugo Lloris has announced his retirement, AC Milan shotstopper,

Mike Maignan could be at the goalpost for France.

The Netherlands: *Oranje*

Ranked seventh in the world, the Netherlands, under the guidance of Ronald Koeman, will be looking to make a statement at Euro 2024. With a rich history and an impressive squad, the Oranje are a force to be reckoned with.

Virgil van Dijk, the Liverpool stalwart and captain of the Dutch side, marshals a defense that includes the likes of Matthijs de Ligt and Nathan Aké. Their solidity at the back provides a solid foundation for the team's attacking endeavors.

In midfield, the presence of Frenkie de Jong and Georginio Wijnaldum provides both creativity and defensive stability, while the likes of

Memphis Depay and Cody Gakpo lead the line with their goalscoring prowess.

Austria: *Das Team*

While not considered one of the favorites, Austria, under the tutelage of Ralf Rangnick, should not be underestimated. Rangnick, known as the "godfather" of modern German football, has instilled a pressing and attacking philosophy that could prove to be a thorn in the side of their group opponents.

David Alaba, the captain and most capped player for Austria, provides invaluable experience and leadership at the heart of the defense. Complemented by the likes of Stefan Posch and Maximilian Wöber, Austria's backline is solid and resolute.

In midfield, the duo of Xaver Schlager and Marcel Sabitzer offer a perfect blend of defensive solidity and creative flair, while the likes of Michael Gregoritsch and Marko Arnautović pose a constant goal threat up front.

Poland: The White-Reds

Led by the legendary Robert Lewandowski, Poland will be a force to be reckoned with in Group D. Lewandowski, the team's captain and all-time top scorer, is a prolific goalscorer who can single-handedly decide the outcome of matches.

However, Poland is more than just Lewandowski. The midfield trio of Piotr Zieliński, Kamil Grosicki, and Przemysław Frankowski provide creativity and industry, while the defense, marshaled by the experienced Jan Bednarek and Bartosz Bereszyński, offers a solid foundation.

Under the guidance of Michał Probierz, Poland will be aiming to build on their impressive qualifying campaign and make a deep run in the tournament.

Head-to-Head Battles
France and the Netherlands have a long-standing rivalry, with the Dutch holding a slight edge in recent encounters. However, the French will be eager to assert their dominance and avenge their losses.

Austria and Poland have also had their fair share of battles, with both teams displaying a tenacity and determination that could make their clashes some of the most fiercely contested in the group.

The Dutch and Austrian teams have a history of closely fought matches, with the last encounter ending in a 2-0 victory for the Netherlands at Euro 2020. However, with both teams having evolved since then, the upcoming matches could present a different storyline.

Given the strength and depth of all four teams, predicting the outcome of Group D is a daunting task. France and the Netherlands are undoubtedly the favorites to progress to the knockout stage, but Austria and Poland will be no pushovers.

If France and the Netherlands live up to their billing and perform to their full potential, they should secure the top two spots in the group. However, if either of them falters or underestimates their opponents, the door could open for Austria or Poland to cause a major upset.

The tactical battles in Group D will be fascinating to watch. France and the Netherlands are likely to employ variations of the 4-3-3 formation, with a focus on possession-based football and quick transitions.

Austria, under Rangnick's influence, could adopt a high-pressing style, looking to disrupt their opponents' rhythm and create opportunities through turnovers in dangerous areas.

Poland, on the other hand, may opt for a more pragmatic approach, looking to soak up pressure and hit teams on the counter-attack, exploiting Lewandowski's lethal finishing ability.

Beyond the on-field battles, there are several intriguing storylines that add depth and context to this group.

Didier Deschamps, the French manager, is aiming to cement his legacy by leading his team to another European Championship triumph. His tactical acumen and man-management skills will be put to the test against formidable opponents.

Ronald Koeman, the Dutch coach, is no stranger to success, having won numerous accolades as a player and manager. His ability to get the best out of his talented squad could be the key to the Netherlands' success.

Ralf Rangnick's appointment as the Austrian manager has raised eyebrows and expectations.

His innovative tactics and pressing philosophy have the potential to cause headaches for the more established teams in the group.

Michał Probierz, the Polish manager, will be looking to guide his team to new heights and potentially secure their first-ever European Championship triumph. His ability to galvanize the squad and get the best out of Lewandowski could be the difference-maker.

As we look ahead to Euro 2024, it's worth reflecting on some of the memorable matches and achievements that have shaped the narratives of these teams.

France's triumphs at Euro 1984 and Euro 2000, where they lifted the trophy on home soil, are etched in the annals of football history. Their breathtaking performances and the individual brilliance of players like Michel Platini and Zinedine Zidane have left an indelible mark on the game.

The Netherlands' victory at Euro 1988, where they defeated the Soviet Union in the final, remains one of the most celebrated achievements in Dutch football. Marco van Basten's iconic volley in that final is still regarded as one of the greatest goals in European Championship history.

Austria's best performance at the European Championships came in 2008 and 2020, when they reached the Round of 16. While they have yet to achieve a breakthrough at this level, their participation in four tournaments is a testament to their consistent efforts.

Poland's quarter-final appearance at Euro 2016, where they were ultimately eliminated by eventual champions Portugal, was a milestone in their football journey. Robert Lewandowski's goals and the team's fighting spirit during that campaign secured their names in Polish football folklore.

5.4 **Group E Analysis**

The Group E of Euro 2024 promises to be a great affair, with heavyweights Belgium and Ukraine joining forces with Romania and Slovakia. This quartet of nations brings an array of talent, tactics, and ambitions to the fore, setting the stage for a riveting battle to secure progression to the knockout rounds.

The Complete Fan's Companion to EURO 2024

At the helm of the Belgian juggernaut is the tactically astute Domenico Tedesco. Hailing from Italy but with a wealth of experience across various European leagues, Tedesco has instilled a pragmatic yet attacking brand of football within the Red Devils' ranks. His philosophy of maintaining a compact defensive shape while unleashing the creative prowess of his star-studded attacking unit has yielded impressive results, propelling Belgium to the third spot in the FIFA rankings.

Spearheading the Belgian offensive is the formidable duo of Kevin De Bruyne and Romelu Lukaku. De Bruyne, the talismanic midfielder, orchestrates the team's rhythm with his pinpoint passing and intelligent movement, while Lukaku's physicality and clinical finishing make him a

The Complete Fan's Companion to EURO 2024

constant threat to opposing defenses. Complemented by the likes of Youri Tielemans, Arsenal's Leandro Trossard, Belgium boasts a squad brimming with quality and experience.

However, the Belgians will face stiff competition from Ukraine, a team that has consistently defied expectations on the international stage. Under the tutelage of Serhiy Rebrov, a former prolific striker himself, Ukraine has embraced a high-energy, pressing style that has caused headaches for even the most formidable opponents.

Andriy Yarmolenko, the captain and talisman, leads by example with his tireless work rate and creative spark, while the dynamic duo of Viktor Tsyhankov and Chelsea winger, Mykhailo Mudryk provide pace and trickery on the flanks. The rock-solid defensive partnership of Mykola Matviyenko and Illya Zabarnyi forms the backbone of Ukraine's resolute rearguard, ensuring a solid foundation for their attacking forays.

Lurking in the shadows is the ever-dangerous Romania, a team that has consistently punched above its weight on the European stage. Under the watchful eye of Edward Iordănescu, a manager renowned for his tactical acumen and man-management skills, Romania has cultivated a balanced and disciplined approach that emphasizes collective effort over individual brilliance.

The experienced Nicolae Stanciu pulls the strings in midfield, orchestrating the team's rhythm and providing a steady supply of service to the dynamic strike partnership of George Pușcaș and Denis Alibec. The defensive duo of Andrei Burcă and Ionuț Nedelcearu offers a formidable barrier, complemented by the goalkeeping prowess of the ever-reliable Florin Niță.

Rounding out the group is Slovakia, a team with a rich footballing tradition and a never-say-die attitude. Led by Francesco Calzona, a rising managerial talent who has already made his mark in various European leagues, Slovakia's approach is built on a solid defensive foundation and swift counter-attacking play.

Milan Škriniar, the talismanic captain, marshals the backline with a commanding presence, while the midfield trio of Juraj Kucka, Ondrej Duda, and Patrik Hrošovský provide industry, creativity, and tactical discipline. Up front, the experienced Róbert Mak and the dynamic Róbert Boženík offer a potent goal-scoring threat, capable of causing problems for any defense on their day.

As the group stage unfolds, each match promises to be a captivating encounter, with the teams' contrasting styles and philosophies adding an extra layer of intrigue. The head-to-head battles between these nations will undoubtedly shape the narrative, with historic rivalries and recent clashes providing ample context for the upcoming battles.

Belgium and Ukraine have locked horns on several occasions, with their most recent encounter resulting in a hard-fought 1-1 draw in the UEFA Nations League in 2018. The Belgians will be wary of Ukraine's relentless pressing and counter-attacking prowess, while the Ukrainians will be eager to exploit any defensive lapses from their illustrious opponents.

Romania's encounters with Belgium have been few and far between, but their last meeting in 2012 saw the Romanians emerge victorious in a thrilling 2-1 friendly clash. The Belgians will be hungry for revenge, but Romania's resilience and tactical discipline cannot be underestimated.

Slovakia's battles with Belgium have often been closely contested affairs, with their most recent meeting in 2013 resulting in a narrow 2-1 victory for the Red Devils. The Slovaks will undoubtedly relish the opportunity to avenge that defeat and showcase their progress on the grand stage of the European Championship.

The historical encounters between Ukraine and Romania have been particularly enthralling, with both nations trading blows in a series of high-scoring affairs. Their most recent clash in 2016 saw Ukraine emerge victorious in a pulsating 4-3 encounter, setting the stage for another mouth-watering clash in Euro 2024.

Slovakia and Ukraine have also engaged in several intriguing battles, with their most recent encounter in 2018 resulting in a resounding 4-1 victory for the Slovaks. However, the ever-improving Ukrainians will be eager to turn the tables and assert their dominance in this highly anticipated rematch.

Finally, the encounters between Romania and Slovakia have often been tight and cagey affairs, with both teams displaying a healthy respect for their opponents' strengths. Their most recent meeting in 2013 ended in a hard-fought 1-1 draw, setting the stage for another intriguing tactical battle in Euro 2024.

As the group stage progresses, the permutations and possibilities will become increasingly complex, with each result holding the potential to reshape the narrative and redefine the trajectories of these teams. The road to the knockout rounds will be arduous, with every point and every goal potentially proving pivotal in determining the ultimate fate of these nations.

5.5 **Group F Analysis**

This group features Portugal, the 2016 European champions, along with Turkey, the Czech

Republic, and Georgia, a team making its debut at a major tournament. With a perfect blend of experience, flair, and underdogs, this group promises to be a captivating spectacle for soccer enthusiasts worldwide.

Portugal: The 2016 Champions Aim for Glory

As the defending champions, Portugal enters the tournament as one of the favorites. Led by the indomitable Cristiano Ronaldo, who continues to defy age at 39, this team boasts a wealth of experience and talent. Under the guidance of Roberto Martínez, the team's new head coach, Portugal will be looking to stamp their authority from the outset.

Martínez, a seasoned tactician, has already left his mark on the Portuguese squad, instilling a free-flowing attacking style of play. With players like Bruno Fernandes, João Félix, and Rafael Leão in the ranks, Portugal's offensive prowess is undeniable. However, their defense, marshaled by veterans like Pepe and João Cancelo, cannot be overlooked either.

Interestingly, Portugal's path to the Euro 2024 has been nothing short of remarkable. They breezed through their qualifying campaign, winning all ten matches and setting records for most goals scored and fewest goals conceded. This dominant display serves as a warning to their group stage opponents, who will have to be at their very best to contain the Portuguese juggernaut.

Turkey: The Dark Horses with a Point to Prove
Turkey, under the tutelage of Vincenzo Montella, will be looking to make a statement at Euro 2024.

The Italian tactician has assembled a talented squad, blending youth and experience, with the likes of Hakan Çalhanoğlu, Enes Ünal, and the promising youngster Arda Güler leading the charge.

Turkey's road to the Euros was not without its challenges, as they had to navigate a tough qualifying group that included Croatia and Wales. However, their fighting spirit shone through, securing their place in the tournament with a decisive 4-0 victory over Latvia in the final qualifying match. They eventually came out top of their group.

With a FIFA ranking of 40th, Turkey may not be among the favorites, but their recent encounters with Portugal have been fiercely contested. The two sides have a long-standing rivalry, and their clashes have often been marked by intense battles and dramatic finishes. This history adds an extra layer of intrigue to their upcoming group stage clash, which could prove to be a pivotal moment in determining the outcome of the group.

The Czech Republic: The Underdogs with a Proven Track Record

The Czech Republic, under the guidance of Ivan Hašek, will be looking to punch above their weight in Group F. Despite being considered underdogs, the Czechs have a proven track record on the big stage, having finished as runners-up at Euro 1996, shortly after the dissolution of Czechoslovakia.

With a solid squad featuring the likes of Patrik Schick, Tomáš Souček, and Adam Hložek, the

Czechs possess the quality to cause upsets. Their recent friendly victories over Norway and Armenia have instilled confidence within the camp, and they will be eager to carry that momentum into the tournament.

Interestingly, the Czech Republic has a mixed history against Portugal and Turkey. While they have enjoyed some memorable victories against the Portuguese, including a 1-0 triumph at Euro 1996, their encounters with Turkey have been more challenging, with the Turks holding a slight edge in recent meetings.

Georgia: The Debutants with Unbridled Enthusiasm

For Georgia, Euro 2024 represents a momentous occasion, as they make their debut in a major tournament. Under the guidance of Willy Sagnol, the Georgian squad will be brimming with enthusiasm and determination to make their mark on the big stage.

Sagnol, a former French international, has instilled a disciplined approach within the Georgian ranks, which was evident in their successful qualifying campaign. Led by the experienced duo of Guram Kashia and Jaba Kankava, and bolstered by the emerging talent of Khvicha Kvaratskhelia, Georgia will be eager to prove their mettle against the established giants of European football.

While Georgia may be the underdogs of the group, their lack of pressure and the opportunity to showcase their abilities on the grandest stage could work in their favor. Their recent victories over Greece and Luxembourg have given them a boost of confidence, and they will be looking to cause a few upsets in the group stage.

The matches in Group F will be played across some of Germany's iconic stadiums, adding a touch of grandeur to the proceedings. The BVB Stadion Dortmund, home to the famous Borussia Dortmund, will host two matches, including Turkey's opener against Georgia. The Volksparkstadion in Hamburg and the Arena AufSchalke in Gelsenkirchen will also play host to group stage encounters, providing a perfect backdrop for the action to unfold.

Group F promises to be a melting pot of intriguing storylines. The long-standing rivalry between Portugal and Turkey will undoubtedly add spice to their clash, with both teams vying for bragging rights and a crucial upper hand in the group.

For Georgia, their debut at a major tournament is a historic moment, and their encounters against the established powerhouses will be a true test of their mettle. Can they pull off a surprise or two and etch their names in the annals of Euro history?

Meanwhile, the Czech Republic will be aiming to recapture the glory days of their Euro 1996 campaign, where they defied odds to reach the final. With a talented squad at their disposal, they will be hoping to spring a few surprises and secure a coveted spot in the knockout stages.

Predicting the outcome of Group F is a daunting task, as each team brings its own set of strengths and uncertainties to the table. However, based on their recent form, pedigree, and squad depth, Portugal emerges as the favorites to top the group.

Turkey, with their blend of experience and youthful exuberance, could potentially secure the second spot, setting up a fierce battle with the Czech Republic for that coveted position. The Czechs, however, cannot be discounted, as their underdog status and proven track record at major tournaments could fuel their ambitions.

As for Georgia, while their chances of progressing to the knockout stages may seem slim, their presence alone promises to add an extra layer of excitement and unpredictability to the group. A few spirited performances and potential upsets could make their Euro 2024 debut a memorable one.

Group F at Euro 2024 promises to be a captivating spectacle, filled with high-stakes clashes, historic debuts, and redemption tales. As the action unfolds on the pitches of Germany, soccer enthusiasts worldwide will be treated to a tantalizing display of skill, determination, and the relentless pursuit of glory that defines the beautiful game.

The Complete Fan's Companion to EURO 2024

Chapter 6: Germany Likely Team Profile

According to my research and analysis, Germany coach Julian Nagelsmann is likely to announce this list of players for the German national team. For goalkeepers, he will probably select Manuel Neuer (Bayern Munich), Marc-André ter Stegen (Barcelona), Alexander Nübel (Stuttgart), and Oliver Baumann (Hoffenheim). The defenders chosen may include Jonathan Tah (Bayer Leverkusen), Nico Schlotterbeck (Borussia Dortmund), Robin Koch (Eintracht Frankfurt), Maximilian Mittelstädt (Stuttgart), Waldemar Anton (Stuttgart), Antonio Rüdiger (Real Madrid), David Raum (RB Leipzig), and Benjamin Henrichs (RB Leipzig). In midfield, the invitees could be Aleksander Pavlovic (Bayern Munich), Robert

The Complete Fan's Companion to EURO 2024

Andrich (Bayer Leverkusen), Joshua Kimmich, Pascal Groß (Brighton and Hove Albion), Ilkay Gundogan (Barcelona), Florian Wirtz, Jamal Musiala (Bayern Munich), and Toni Kroos (Real Madrid). For attackers, the coach may call up Niclas Füllkrug (Borussia Dortmund), Chris Führich (Stuttgart), Leroy Sané (Bayern Munich), Kai Havertz (Arsenal), Deniz Undav (Stuttgart), Maximilian Beier (Hoffenheim), and Thomas Müller (Bayern Munich). Germany's group contains Scotland, Hungary, and Switzerland. The team will play warm-up games against Ukraine and Greece before the tournament.

The Complete Fan's Companion to EURO 2024

Chapter 7: Tournament Schedule

The European Championship 2024 group stage fixtures get underway on June 14th, 2024 according to UEFA's schedule. In Group A, the host nation Germany will play their opening match against Scotland at 21:00 on June 14th at the Fußball Arena München in Munich. The following day, June 15th, will see Hungary face Switzerland at 15:00 at the Cologne Stadium in Cologne. Germany and Hungary will then meet on June 19th at 18:00 at the Stuttgart Arena, while Scotland takes on Switzerland later that evening at 21:00 back in Cologne. Germany's final group game is against Switzerland on June 23rd at 21:00 at the Frankfurt Arena, with Scotland playing Hungary at the same time in Stuttgart.

The Complete Fan's Companion to EURO 2024

Group B kicks off on June 15th with Spain vs Croatia at 18:00 in Berlin's Olympiastadion, followed by Italy against Albania at 21:00 at the BVB Stadion Dortmund. Croatia and Albania meet on June 19th at 15:00 in Hamburg, before Spain faces Italy at 21:00 on June 20th in Gelsenkirchen. Albania then plays Spain on June 24th at 21:00 in Düsseldorf, with Croatia taking on Italy simultaneously in Leipzig.

Slovenia and Denmark open Group C on June 16th at 18:00 in Stuttgart, while Serbia plays England at 21:00 that day in Gelsenkirchen. Slovenia meets Serbia on June 20th at 15:00 in Munich, as Denmark faces England at 18:00 in Frankfurt. England's final group match is versus Slovenia on June 25th at 21:00 in Cologne, with Denmark playing Serbia concurrently in Munich.

The Complete Fan's Companion to EURO 2024

In Group D, the first matches are on June 16th. Poland will play the Netherlands at 3pm in Hamburg. The next day, June 17th, Austria will face France at 9pm in Düsseldorf. A few days later on June 21st, Poland takes on Austria at 6pm in Berlin. That same night, the Netherlands plays France at 9pm in Leipzig. Then on June 25th, there are two more Group D games - the Netherlands versus Austria at 6pm in Berlin, and France against Poland at 6pm in Dortmund.

In Group E, the first games are on June 17th. Romania meets Ukraine at 3pm in Munich, while Belgium plays Slovakia at 6pm in Frankfurt. Four days later on June 21st, Slovakia goes up against Ukraine at 3pm in Düsseldorf. The next day, June 22nd, Belgium faces Romania at 9pm in Cologne. Towards the end of the group stage on June 26th,

The Complete Fan's Companion to EURO 2024

Slovakia takes on Romania at 6pm in Frankfurt, and later that night Ukraine plays Belgium at 6pm in Stuttgart.

Group F kicks off on June 18th with Turkey against Georgia at 6pm in Dortmund, followed by Portugal versus Czech Republic at 9pm in Leipzig. Then on June 22nd, Georgia meets Czech Republic at 3pm in Hamburg, while Turkey plays Portugal at 6pm back in Dortmund. The final Group F games are on June 26th - Georgia vs Portugal at 9pm in Gelsenkirchen, and Czech Republic against Turkey at 9pm in Hamburg.

The teams that finish third in their groups may still advance to the next round depending on points earned, goal difference, goals scored, wins, disciplinary record, and their overall European qualifiers ranking. The exact criteria will determine which third-placed teams move on.

7.1 Knockout Stage Overview

The knockout phase of UEFA Euro 2024 kicks off after the group stage concludes. If any match is level at the end of regulation time, it will go into extra time consisting of two 15-minute periods. Should the scores remain tied after extra time, a penalty shoot-out will determine the winner. There will be no third place play-off match in this tournament.

The specific match-ups for the round of 16 involving the third-placed teams depend on which four third-placed teams qualify from their respective groups. The round of 16 gets underway on 29 June 2024 at 18:00 local time in Berlin, with the runner-up of Group A facing the runner-up of Group B. Later that evening at 21:00, the winner of Group A takes on the runner-up of Group C in Dortmund.

The next day, 30 June, has two more round of 16 ties - at 18:00 in Gelsenkirchen, the winner of Group C meets one of the third-placed teams, while at 21:00 in Cologne, the winner of Group B faces another third-placed side.

On 1 July at 18:00 in Düsseldorf, the runner-up of Group D plays the runner-up of Group E. Then at 21:00 in Frankfurt, the winner of Group F clashes with a third-placed team. The round of 16 concludes on 2 July, with the winner of Group E versus a third-placed team at 18:00 in Munich,

The Complete Fan's Companion to EURO 2024

followed by the winner of Group D against the runner-up of Group F at 21:00 in Leipzig.

The quarter-finals take place across two days - 5 July has matches at 18:00 and 21:00 in Stuttgart and Hamburg respectively. 6 July also witnesses quarter-final ties at 18:00 in Düsseldorf and 21:00 in Berlin.

The semi-finals are single matches, with the first one on 9 July at 21:00 in Munich, while the second semi-final is scheduled for 10 July at 21:00 in Dortmund.

The UEFA Euro 2024 final, where the new European champion will be crowned, will be played on 14 July 2024 at the iconic Olympiastadion in Berlin at 21:00 local time. All

The Complete Fan's Companion to EURO 2024

match timings are per the Central European Summer Time (CEST) zone, which is UTC+2.

The Complete Fan's Companion to EURO 2024

Chapter 8: Germany Hosting History at EURO

Germany has a long history of hosting the UEFA European Football Championship, also known as the Euros. This prestigious tournament is organized by UEFA and held every four years, featuring the top national teams from across Europe.

From 1960 to 1976, the host nation for the Euros was decided from among the four semi-finalists of the previous tournament. However, this system changed in 1980, and since then, the host nation has automatically qualified for the final tournament, except in 2020 when every country had to go through the qualification process due to the COVID-19 pandemic.

The Complete Fan's Companion to EURO 2024

Germany has had the honor of hosting the Euros on multiple occasions. They first hosted the tournament in 1988 when it was known as UEFA Euro 1988. This was the eighth edition of the European Championship, and it took place in West Germany from June 10 to June 25, 1988.

As the host nation, West Germany automatically qualified for the final tournament. The other seven teams that qualified were Denmark, the Soviet Union, England, the Republic of Ireland, Italy, Spain, and the Netherlands. It was the first time the Republic of Ireland had qualified for a major tournament.

In the bidding process, Germany's proposal beat out a joint bid from Sweden, Norway, and Denmark, as well as a bid from England. The decision to award the hosting rights to Germany was influenced by the country's strong infrastructure, extensive experience in hosting major sporting events, and the passion of its football fans.

Eight stadiums across eight host cities in West Germany were used as venues for UEFA Euro 1988. These included the Olympiastadion in Munich, the Parkstadion in Gelsenkirchen, the Volksparkstadion in Hamburg, the Waldstadion in Frankfurt, the Rheinstadion in Düsseldorf, the Niedersachsenstadion in Hanover, the Neckarstadion in Stuttgart, and the Müngersdorfer Stadion in Cologne.

The tournament format consisted of a group stage followed by knockout rounds. The eight teams were divided into two groups of four, with the top two teams from each group advancing to the semi-finals.

In Group 1, West Germany and Italy progressed to the semi-finals, while Spain and Denmark were eliminated. In Group 2, the Soviet Union and the Netherlands made it to the semi-finals, while the Republic of Ireland and England were knocked out.

The first semi-final saw West Germany take on the Netherlands in a highly anticipated match between the two neighboring nations. The Dutch emerged victorious with a 2-1 win, thanks to a late goal from Marco van Basten. This marked the first time the Netherlands had defeated West Germany in a competitive match.

In the other semi-final, the Soviet Union pulled off a surprising 2-0 victory over the favored Italian side, setting up a final showdown against the Netherlands.

The final was played on June 25, 1988, at the Olympiastadion in Munich. The Netherlands put on a dominant performance, defeating the Soviet Union 2-0 with goals from Ruud Gullit and Marco van Basten. Van Basten's spectacular volley goal is widely regarded as one of the greatest goals in European Championship history.

UEFA Euro 1988 was a memorable tournament, with a few notable achievements. It was the first time the Netherlands had won the European Championship, and it was also the last time the Soviet Union competed in the tournament before its dissolution in 1991. Additionally, the tournament did not witness a single red card, goalless draw, or knockout match going to extra time or penalties – a rare occurrence in a major football tournament.

Top Goalscorers at UEFA Euro 1988:

The top goalscorer of the tournament was Marco van Basten of the Netherlands, who scored 5 goals. Oleh Protasov of the Soviet Union and Rudi Völler of West Germany each scored 2 goals.

A total of 34 goals were scored across the 15 matches played, averaging 2.27 goals per match.

Awards:

UEFA named their Team of the Tournament after the final, which included:

Goalkeeper: Hans van Breukelen (Netherlands)

Defenders: Giuseppe Bergomi (Italy), Paolo Maldini (Italy), Ronald Koeman (Netherlands), Frank Rijkaard (Netherlands)

Midfielders: Giuseppe Giannini (Italy), Jan Wouters (Netherlands), Lothar Matthäus (West Germany)

Forwards: Gianluca Vialli (Italy), Ruud Gullit (Netherlands), Marco van Basten (Netherlands)

Euro 2020

Euro 2020 was the 16th edition of the UEFA European Championship. It was the quadrennial international men's football championship

The Complete Fan's Companion to EURO 2024

organized by UEFA (Union of European Football Associations).

To celebrate the 60th anniversary of the European Championship, UEFA decided to host the tournament across multiple nations instead of having just one or two host countries. This unique format made Euro 2020 the second senior international tournament in history, after the 2007 AFC Asian Cup, to have more than two co-host nations.

Initially, 13 venues across 13 countries were selected to host matches. However, Brussels was later dropped as a host city in December 2017 after plans for the Eurostadium were abandoned. Dublin was also removed as a host in April 2021 because there was no guarantee spectators could attend matches due to COVID-19 restrictions.

The Complete Fan's Companion to EURO 2024

Germany was one of the successful bidders and was awarded the right to host matches in the city of Munich at the Allianz Arena. The prestigious 70,000-capacity stadium was chosen as one of the 12 host venues across 11 countries for Euro 2020.

The tournament was originally scheduled for June-July 2020 but had to be postponed by a year due to the COVID-19 pandemic sweeping across Europe. However, it retained the name "UEFA Euro 2020" despite being played in 2021. Other unique rules implemented included allowing teams to make five substitutions per game instead of three, and the use of video assistant referees (VAR) for the first time in the tournament's history.

The Complete Fan's Companion to EURO 2024

As one of the top-seeded nations, the German national team automatically qualified for the final tournament as hosts. They were drawn into Group F alongside world champions France, defending European champions Portugal, and Hungary.

Munich's Allianz Arena hosted all three of Germany's group stage matches as well as a quarter-final tie. The first match saw Germany suffer a narrow 1-0 defeat against France, with Mats Hummels scoring an unfortunate own goal.

In their second game, Germany bounced back with an impressive 4-2 victory over Portugal. Cristiano Ronaldo gave Portugal the lead, but Germany responded through own goals from Ruben Dias and Raphael Guerreiro. Kai Havertz and Robin Gosens then added two more goals for Germany.

The final group game was a dramatic 2-2 draw against Hungary. Adam Szalai and Andras Schafer scored for Hungary, but Havertz and Leon Goretzka equalized for Germany to secure qualification for the knockout rounds.

In the round of 16, Germany faced old rivals England at Wembley Stadium. Despite a strong performance, Germany's tournament came to an end with a 2-0 defeat. Raheem Sterling and Harry Kane scored the goals that sent England through to the quarter-finals.

Munich's Allianz Arena also hosted one of the quarter-final ties between Belgium and Italy. It was a high-quality encounter that saw Italy edge out Belgium 2-1, with goals from Lorenzo Insigne and Nicolo Barella canceling out Romelu Lukaku's penalty.

Euro 2020 was a successful and entertaining tournament. There were a total of 142 goals scored across the 51 matches, averaging 2.78 goals per game – the highest goal average since the introduction of the group stage format in 1976.

Eleven own goals were scored, more than all previous European Championships combined. Portugal's Cristiano Ronaldo became the all-time top scorer in European Championship history with 14 goals.

The top scorers at Euro 2020 were Cristiano Ronaldo of Portugal and Patrik Schick of the

Czech Republic, who both netted 5 goals each. Belgium's Romelu Lukaku, England's Harry Kane, France's Karim Benzema, and Sweden's Emil Forsberg all scored 4 goals.

After the final between Italy and England ended 1-1 after extra time, Italy emerged as champions for the second time after winning the penalty shootout 3-2. Their victory came exactly on the 39th anniversary of their 1982 World Cup triumph.

Italy goalkeeper Gianluigi Donnarumma was named Player of the Tournament, becoming the first-ever goalkeeper to receive this award. Spain's Pedri was named the Young Player of the Tournament.

The Complete Fan's Companion to EURO 2024

UEFA's technical observers selected their Team of the Tournament, which included five Italian players: Donnarumma, Leonardo Bonucci, Leonardo Spinazzola, Jorginho and Federico Chiesa. Other notable inclusions were England's Kyle Walker, Harry Maguire and Raheem Sterling, Belgium's Romelu Lukaku, Denmark's Pierre-Emile Højbjerg and Spain's Pedri.

Patrik Schick's stunning long-range effort against Scotland was voted the Goal of the Tournament by fans in an online poll.

Despite some controversies, such as the Greenpeace protester incident before France-Germany and the debate over illuminating Munich's stadium in rainbow colors for a political statement, and Manuel Neuer's wearing of rainbow armband, Euro 2020 was widely praised for its entertaining football, quick refereeing decisions, and judicious use of VAR technology.

As one of the host cities, Munich and the Allianz Arena played a pivotal role in delivering a successful and memorable UEFA Euro 2020 tournament. Germany's hosting responsibilities marked another milestone in the country's rich footballing heritage and organizational capabilities for major sporting events.

UEFA's decision to spread Euro 2020 across multiple European cities turned out to be a fitting celebration of the tournament's 60th anniversary, despite the logistical challenges posed by the COVID-19 pandemic. The pan-European format allowed fans across the continent to experience the thrill of hosting Europe's biggest football spectacle.

Euro 2024

This is Germany's next opportunity to host the Euros came in 2024, when they were selected as the host nation for the 24th edition of the tournament. This marked the third time Germany had been chosen to host the prestigious event, having previously hosted in 1988(as West Germany), 2020 (as Joint hosting), and 2024.

The tournament is scheduled to take place from June 14 to July 14, 2024, with matches being played across ten stadiums in ten different cities across Germany. These venues include the Allianz Arena in Munich, the Olympiastadion in

The Complete Fan's Companion to EURO 2024

Berlin, the Signal Iduna Park in Dortmund, the Red Bull Arena in Leipzig, the Veltins-Arena in Gelsenkirchen, the Mercedes-Benz Arena in Stuttgart, the Rhein-Energie-Stadion in Cologne, the Volksparkstadion in Hamburg, the Frankfurt Stadium in Frankfurt, and the Arena AufSchalke in Gelsenkirchen.

As the host nation, Germany automatically qualified for UEFA Euro 2024, marking their 14th appearance in the European Championship. The other 23 participating teams had to go through a rigorous qualification process, which began in March 2022 and concluded in November 2023.

The tournament format for UEFA Euro 2024 consists of a group stage followed by knockout rounds. The 24 teams are divided into six groups of four, with the top two teams from each group automatically progressing to the round of 16, along with the four best third-placed teams.

The round of 16 matches will be followed by the quarter-finals, semi-finals, and the final, which is scheduled to take place on July 14, 2024, at the Olympiastadion in Berlin.

As the host nation, Germany has high hopes and expectations for a successful tournament on home soil. The country boasts a rich football heritage, having won four FIFA World Cup titles and three European Championships (as West Germany in 1972 and 1980, and as a unified Germany in 1996).

The German national team, known as *Die Mannschaft*, will be led by head coach Julian Nagelsmann, who took over the role in

The Complete Fan's Companion to EURO 2024

September 2023. The team features a blend of experienced veterans and promising young talents, including players like Marc-Andre Ter Stegen, Thomas Müller, Joshua Kimmich, Leroy Sanè, and Kai Havertz.

German fans are eagerly awaiting the opportunity to cheer on their national team on home soil and witness the best teams and players from across Europe compete for the coveted European Championship trophy. The tournament is expected to be a grand celebration of football, bringing together fans from all over the continent in a spirit of unity and sportsmanship.

Germany's hosting of UEFA Euro 2024 marks another milestone in the country's rich footballing history and its commitment to organizing world-class sporting events. With

The Complete Fan's Companion to EURO 2024

state-of-the-art stadiums, passionate fans, and well-oiled organizational machinery, Germany is poised to deliver an unforgettable and successful European Championship tournament.

The Complete Fan's Companion to EURO 2024

Chapter 9: German Legends

Germany has produced many legendary footballers throughout history. The German national team is one of the most successful in the world, having won the World Cup four times in 1954, 1974, 1990, and 2014. Germany has featured numerous world-class players who have left a lasting mark on the sport. From players like Franz Beckenbauer, Gerd Müller, and Lothar Matthäus who were part of Germany's World Cup triumphs, to more recent stars like Oliver Kahn, Michael Ballack, Bastian Schweinsteiger, Philipp Lahm, Miroslav Klose, Lukas Podolski, Thomas Müller, and Manuel Neuer - the talent pipeline from this football-obsessed nation seems endlessly stocked with stars. Some of Germany's all-time greats are household names globally. Players like Franz Beckenbauer, who won the World Cup as both a player and manager, have etched their names in football folklore. Strikers like Gerd Muller and Miroslav Klose are among the highest goalscorers in World Cup history. In goal, Oliver Kahn was named best player at the 2002 World Cup. Germany's football legends span generations and embody the talent, mental strength and winning mentality that has made *Die Mannschaft* such a force over the decades.

Lothar Matthäus

Lothar Matthäus is considered one of the greatest German footballers of all time. He was a versatile and complete player who excelled as a box-to-box midfielder known for his perceptive passing, positioning, tackling, and powerful shooting with either foot.

Matthäus holds the record for most appearances for the German national team with 150 caps over a 20-year international career from 1980 to 2000. He is one of only six male players to have played in five different FIFA World Cup tournaments (1982, 1986, 1990, 1994, 1998). The others are Antonio Carbajal, Rafael Márquez, Lionel Messi, Cristiano Ronaldo, and Andrés Guardado.

Matthäus made his international debut for West Germany at the 1980 European Championship, which his team won. At the 1982 World Cup in Spain, he appeared as a substitute in group stage matches as West Germany reached the final before losing to Italy.

By the 1986 World Cup in Mexico, Matthäus had become a regular starter. He scored the winner against Morocco in the round of 16. In the final against Argentina, he was tasked with man-marking Diego Maradona, though Maradona set up the winning goal for Argentina late on as West Germany lost 3-2.

Captaining West Germany at Euro 1988, Matthäus scored from the penalty spot against the Netherlands in the semi-finals before they lost 2-1. At the 1990 World Cup in Italy, Matthäus led his side to their third World Cup triumph, scoring four goals including two in the opening 4-1 win over Yugoslavia.

In the quarter-finals, he netted the only goal from the penalty spot against Czechoslovakia. West Germany then beat Argentina 1-0 in the final rematch in Rome, with Matthäus lifting the trophy as captain. It was West Germany's last major tournament before reunification with East Germany.

Matthäus missed Euro 1992 due to injury as the reunified Germany lost the final to Denmark. At the 1994 World Cup in the USA, he operated as a sweeper and scored a penalty against Bulgaria in the quarter-finals, equaling the then-record of 21 World Cup appearances. However, Bulgaria came from behind to win 2-1.

Though expected to retire after 1994, Matthäus surprisingly returned for the 1998 World Cup in France, becoming only the second player at that time to play in five different World Cups, matching Carbajal's record. He featured in all of Germany's matches until they were eliminated by

Croatia in the quarter-finals, setting a new World Cup appearances record of 25 games.

Matthäus earned his final three caps at Euro 2000, with his 150th and last international cap coming against Portugal as Germany exited in the group stage. His two-decade international career spanned an incredible nine major tournaments from Euro 1980 to Euro 2000.

In addition to his World Cup success in 1990, Matthäus won Euro 1980 with West Germany and finished as a World Cup runner-up in 1982 and 1986. At club level, he won seven Bundesliga titles with Bayern Munich as well as lifting the 1990 Ballon d'Or.

Matthäus was renowned for his leadership, winning mentality, determination and commanding presence on the pitch. He was inducted into the FIFA 100 list of greatest living players chosen by Pele. Diego Maradona called Matthäus the best rival he had ever had.

Matthäus typically played as a box-to-box midfielder early in his career before being converted to a sweeper role late on. He excelled in both positions thanks to his well-rounded skills and ability to read the game. An expert set-piece taker, he combined tackling, passing, shooting ability and stamina.

While not necessarily world-class in any one area individually, Matthäus was highly competent in every facet of the game, allowing him to influence play all over the pitch. This exceptional all-around ability is what made him such a valuable player for both club and country over a career spanning more than two decades at the highest level.

Lothar Matthäus was a legendary German footballer who captained his nation to World Cup glory in 1990 while setting records for World Cup appearances and cementing his status as one of the greatest and most complete midfielders of all time through his longevity, leadership, tenacity and well-rounded skillset. He is Germany's most capped player and one of the select few men's players to feature at five different World Cup tournaments.

Jürgen Klinsmann

Jürgen Klinsmann is considered one of Germany's premier strikers and a true legend of

German football. Born on July 30, 1964 in Göppingen, West Germany, the striker played for several top European clubs including VfB Stuttgart, Inter Milan, Monaco, Tottenham Hotspur, and Bayern Munich.

Klinsmann enjoyed a highly successful international career representing West Germany and the unified German national team. He made 108 appearances for Germany, the fourth-most capped German player ever behind Lothar Matthäus, Miroslav Klose and Lukas Podolski. His 47 goals ranks him fourth on Germany's all-time goal scoring list, only surpassed by the legendary Klose, Gerd Müller and Podolski. Klinsmann's 11 World Cup goals place him sixth on the all-time World Cup scorer's list.

A key part of the West German World Cup winning team in 1990, Klinsmann scored in the 1-0 quarter-final victory over the Netherlands after teammate Rudi Völler was sent off. He played a vital role in Germany's run to the title, defeating Argentina 1-0 in the final. Klinsmann also starred for the unified German side, becoming the first player to score at least 3 goals in 3 consecutive World Cups (1994, 1998) before being joined by Ronaldo and Miroslav Klose.

In addition to the 1990 World Cup triumph, Klinsmann won the 1996 European Championship and claimed a bronze medal at the 1988 Seoul Olympics. He participated in a total of 4 World Cups and 3 European Championships for West Germany/Germany. The first player to score in 3 different Euro tournaments, he is remembered for his diving antics but also for his predatory finishing ability.

Klinsmann's club and individual honors include the Bundesliga top scorer in 1987-88, two-time German Footballer of the Year, a place in the FIFA World Cup All-Star Team in 1990, the FWA Footballer of the Year at Tottenham in 1994-95, and runner-up for the 1995 Ballon d'Or. He was named to the FIFA 100 list of greatest living players in 2004.

Franz Beckenbauer

Franz Beckenbauer, nicknamed "Der Kaiser" (The Emperor), is widely regarded as one of the greatest footballers of all time. He was a versatile player who initially played as a midfielder before making his name as an innovative central defender, often credited with inventing the modern sweeper or libero role.

Beckenbauer had a legendary career for both club and country. At the international level, he earned 103 caps and scored 14 goals for West Germany between 1965 and 1977. He played in three World Cups - 1966, 1970 and 1974. In the 1966 tournament in England, the 20-year-old Beckenbauer starred as West Germany finished runners-up to the hosts. He scored four goals, including twice in the opening 5-0 win over Switzerland. He also netted in the semi-final victory over the Soviet Union as West Germany reached the final before losing to England.

Four years later at the 1970 World Cup in Mexico, Beckenbauer helped West Germany to a third-place finish. He memorably scored a spectacular goal as they came from 2-0 down to beat England 3-2 after extra time in a quarter-final rematch of the 1966 final. However, West Germany then lost the iconic "Game of the Century" semi-final to Italy after Beckenbauer had to play part of the match with a dislocated shoulder.

Beckenbauer's defining moment came at the 1974 World Cup which was hosted by West Germany. As captain, he led his country to their first World Cup triumph thanks in large part to his outstanding leadership and man-marking of Dutch legend Johan Cruyff in the 2-1 win over the Netherlands in the final. Beckenbauer became the first captain to lift the new FIFA World Cup trophy.

In addition to his World Cup heroics, Beckenbauer won the 1972 European Championship with West Germany and was runner-up at the 1976 edition. He was twice named European Footballer of the Year, claiming the Ballon d'Or awards in 1972 and 1976. Beckenbauer is one of only three men, along with Brazil's Mario Zagallo and France's Didier Deschamps, to have won the World Cup as both a player and a manager.

At club level, Beckenbauer was a one-club man for the majority of his career, starring for Bayern Munich from 1964 to 1977. During his time in Bavaria, Bayern won three consecutive European Cups/Champions Leagues from 1974 to 1976, with Beckenbauer being the first player to captain a team to that continental treble.

He later had short stints in the USA with the New York Cosmos and Hamburg in Germany before returning to the Cosmos and retiring as a player in 1983. Beckenbauer's incredible haul of trophies included four Bundesliga titles, four German Cups, one European Cup Winners' Cup, and three European Cups/Champions Leagues.

After hanging up his boots, Beckenbauer moved into management and coaching. His crowning achievement was leading the reunified Germany squad to glory at the 1990 World Cup in Italy, becoming one of the few men to win it as both a player and manager. He was also West Germany's manager when they finished as runners-up at the 1986 World Cup.

Beyond playing and coaching, Beckenbauer had a pivotal role in bringing the 2006 World Cup to

Germany as he led the successful bid and then chaired the organizing committee. His immense contributions to Germany and global football were recognized by his inductions into the World Team of the 20th Century, FIFA 100, and multiple FIFA honors.

Beckenbauer is considered a pioneer and icon of the modern game. He is the only defender in history to win the Ballon d'Or twice. His innovating sweeper role, blending defense with offense, fundamentally changed how central defenders played. Beckenbauer's reading of the game, positioning, tackling, and passing range from the back allowed him to initiate attacks and be a driving force for his teams.

Beckenbauer's personality and aura also separated him from other greats. His confidence, leadership, and regal presence on the pitch earned him the "Der Kaiser" moniker. He embraced big occasions and thrived under pressure, delivering his best performances on the biggest stages like three World Cup tournaments.

Teammates and opponents alike revered Beckenbauer's ability and impact. England's Bobby Charlton praised how Beckenbauer's mere presence deterred opponents from taking him on.

After his career, Beckenbauer worked as a pundit and newspaper columnist for over three decades. He did face legal issues related to allegations of corruption surrounding Germany's 2006 World Cup bid, though charges were ultimately dropped due to the statute of limitations.

When Beckenbauer sadly passed away in January 2024 at age 78, he was mourned across the football world. Beckenbauer left an indelible mark on the game through his trophy-laden playing career, pioneering influence, big-game brilliance, and force of personality and leadership.

Few players dominated at the levels Beckenbauer did over such a lengthy period for both club and country. He was a World Cup hero, European championship winner, Champions League trailblazer, and simply one of the most complete, impactful and iconic footballers in the history of the sport. Franz Beckenbauer will forever be "Der Kaiser " of Germany and world football.

Gerd Müller

Gerd Müller was known as the World's Cup greatest goalscorer. The German was lethalness personified. He simply did what he was paid to do much better than everyone else: score sheer amounts of goals.

Between 1964-1979, Muller helped himself to an eye-watering 563 goals and duly became Bayern Munich's all-time goalscorer, with the majority of people under the impression that it is a record that may never be usurped. Nicknamed 'Der Bomber' for his ability to terrorize defenses with his strength, power and speed, Muller can be considered the greatest goalscorer in German football folklore.

Gerhard "Gerd" Müller was a German professional footballer. A prolific striker, especially in and around the six-yard box, he is widely regarded as one of the greatest goalscorers in the history of the sport. With success at club and international level, he is one of nine players to have won the FIFA World Cup, the UEFA Champions League and the Ballon d'Or.

At international level with West Germany, he scored 68 goals in 62 appearances. At club level, in 15 years with Bayern Munich, he scored 365 goals in 427 Bundesliga matches, becoming the record holder of that league. In 74 European club games he scored 65 goals. Averaging over a goal per game with West Germany, Müller was 21st on the list of all-time international goalscorers, despite playing fewer matches than every other player in the top 48. Among the top scorers, he has the third-highest goal-to-game ratio. He also had the highest ratio of 0.97 goals per game in the European Cup, scoring 34 goals in 35 matches.

Nicknamed "Bomber der Nation" ("the nation's Bomber") or simply "Der Bomber", Müller was named European Footballer of the Year in 1970. After a successful season at Bayern Munich, he scored ten goals at the 1970 FIFA World Cup for West Germany where he received the Golden Boot as top goalscorer, before winning the 1970 Ballon d'Or. In 1972, he won the UEFA European Championship and was the top goalscorer, scoring two goals in the final. Two years later, he scored 4 goals in the 1974 FIFA World Cup, including the winning goal in the final.

Müller held the all-time goal-scoring record in the World Cup with 14 goals for 32 years. In 1999, Müller was ranked ninth in the European Player of the Century election held by the International Federation of Football History & Statistics (IFFHS), and he was voted 13th in the IFFHS' World Player of the Century election. In 2004, Pelé named Müller in the FIFA 100 list of the world's greatest living players.

His international career started in 1966 and ended on 7 July 1974 with victory at the 1974 FIFA World Cup at his home stadium in Munich. He scored the winning goal for the 2–1 victory over Johan Cruyff's Netherlands in the final. His four goals in that tournament and his ten goals at the 1970 FIFA World Cup combined made him the all-time highest FIFA World Cup goalscorer at the time with 14 goals. His record stood until the 2006 tournament, when it was broken by Brazilian striker Ronaldo, who also required more matches than Müller to achieve his tally. Müller also participated in the 1972 European Championship, becoming top scorer with four goals (including two in the final) and winning the Championship with the West German team.

Müller quit playing for West Germany after the 1974 FIFA World Cup triumph following an argument with the German Football Association.

He is widely considered to be one of the greatest goalscorers in the history of football. He is seen as the greatest "goal poacher" in history, with Gary Lineker calling him the ultimate goal poacher. He is one of only two players, alongside Lionel Messi, to have won the FIFA World Cup, the UEFA Champions League, the Ballon d'Or and the European Golden Shoe. After his death in 2021, FC Bayern Munich president Herbert Hainer declared that Müller was the greatest striker there's ever been, while Franz Beckenbauer stated that Müller was the most important player in the history of Bayern Munich.

Müller was short, squat, awkward-looking and not notably fast; he never fitted the conventional idea of a great footballer, but he had lethal acceleration over short distances, a remarkable aerial game, and uncanny goalscoring instincts. His short legs gave him a low center of gravity, so he could turn quickly and with perfect balance in spaces and at speeds that would cause other players to fall over. He also had a knack of scoring in unlikely situations.

Müller used extreme acceleration and deceptive changes of pace to get to loose balls first, and bypass defenders.

Oliver Kahn

Oliver Kahn is one of the most successful German players in recent history. He started his career in the Karlsruher SC Junior team in 1975. Twelve years later, Kahn made his debut match in the professional squad. In 1994, he was transferred to Bayern Munich where he played until the end of his career in 2008. His commanding presence in goal and aggressive style earned him nicknames such as Der Titan ("The Titan") from the press and Vol-kahn-o ("volcano") from fans.

Kahn is one of the most successful German players in recent history, having won eight Bundesliga titles, six DFB-Pokals, the UEFA Cup in 1996, the UEFA Champions League and the

Intercontinental Cup, both achieved in 2001. Regarded as one of the greatest goalkeepers of all time, his individual contributions have earned him a record four consecutive UEFA Best European Goalkeeper awards, as well as three IFFHS World's Best Goalkeeper awards, and two German Footballer of the Year trophies. At the 2002 FIFA World Cup, Kahn became the only goalkeeper in the tournament's history to win the Golden Ball.

Kahn was initially called for the Germany national team as a late back-up for the 1994 FIFA World Cup, but made his first appearance on 23 June 1995 in a victory against Switzerland, after recovering from a cruciate ligament injury. He was a reserve keeper when Germany won the 1996 UEFA European Championship.

Kahn spent the 1998 World Cup on the bench, and became the starting goalkeeper after Köpke's retirement. In 2002, he received the captaincy, succeeding Oliver Bierhoff. Despite low expectations, Germany advanced to the 2002 World Cup final; Kahn conceded only three goals, two in the final loss to Brazil. Playing with torn ligaments, he fumbled a rebounded shot allowing Ronaldo to score. Nevertheless he refused to blame his injury, and was awarded the Golden Ball for best individual performance, the only goalkeeper to win it.

Kahn maintained his number one spot for the 2004 Euros, but Germany were eliminated in the group stage. He gave up his captaincy to Michael Ballack after the tournament. Under new manager Klinsmann, Kahn rotated the number one spot with Jens Lehmann to stimulate competition, before Lehmann was named first-choice for the 2006 World Cup. Kahn stayed on as backup, accepting the decision.

In the 2006 quarter-finals against Argentina, despite their pre-tournament dispute, Kahn openly accepted Klinsmann's decision and embraced and encouraged Lehmann, who made decisive penalty saves. After Germany's semi-final loss to Italy, Kahn was given his final international start in the third place play-off win over Portugal, receiving the captaincy. Following the match, Kahn announced his retirement from the national team with 86 caps, including 49 as captain, though he never won a World Cup, finishing runner-up in 2002 and third in 2006.

Regarded as one of the greatest goalkeepers ever, in addition to his goalkeeping technique, agility, reflexes, distribution, command of area, and shot-stopping abilities, Kahn is admired for the stamina, mental strength, and composure he showed overcoming career pressures. Known for his eccentricity and charismatic leadership from the back calling out defenders, his epithet was "The Titan"; he was frequently nicknamed "King Kahn" for the formidable presence and aggressive playing style he showed in goal.

Oliver Kahn is one of the most successful German goalkeepers in recent history. He won eight Bundesliga titles, six German Cups, the 1996 UEFA Cup, 2001 UEFA Champions League and Intercontinental Cup. His individual honors include four consecutive UEFA Best European Goalkeeper awards, three IFFHS World's Best Goalkeeper awards, and two German Footballer of the Year trophies. At the 2002 World Cup, he became the only goalkeeper ever to win the Golden Ball award.

Kahn made his Germany debut in 1995 after recovering from a cruciate ligament injury. He was an unused reserve as Germany won Euro 1996, and again at the 1998 World Cup before becoming first-choice goalkeeper after Andreas Köpke's retirement. He captained Germany from 2002, leading them surprisingly to the 2002 World Cup final despite low expectations, where despite a costly error, he won the Golden Ball as the tournament's best player, having conceded just three goals.

Though Germany disappointed at Euro 2004, exiting in the group stage, Kahn remained number one until being rotated with Jens Lehmann by new coach Jurgen Klinsmann ahead of the 2006 World Cup, where Lehmann was eventually preferred. Kahn stayed on as backup, embracing the decision. Making his final international appearance as captain in Germany's third-place playoff win over Portugal, Kahn retired after the 2006 World Cup with 86 caps, 49 as captain, though he never won the World Cup, finishing runner-up in 2002 and third in 2006.

In addition to his goalkeeping abilities, Kahn was admired for his leadership, mentality and commanding presence, earning the moniker "The Titan" for his formidable character and aggression in goal. Regarded among the all-time greats, he placed highly in votings for the best goalkeeper of the 21st century and previous 25 years.

Bastian Schweinsteiger

Bastian Schweinsteiger, born 1 August 1984 in Kolbermoor, Germany, is a German football player. He represented Germany from a very young age, playing for the U16, U18, U19 and U21 teams between 2000-2004 before making his senior international debut in 2004 at age 20. Schweinsteiger went on to have an illustrious career with the German national team over the next 12 years, earning 121 caps and scoring 24 goals. His international honors with Germany include winning the 2014 FIFA World Cup in Brazil, finishing third at the 2006 World Cup in Germany and 2010 World Cup in South Africa. He was also part of the Germany sides that were runners-up at the 2008 European Championship in Austria and Switzerland, and third place at both the 2005 FIFA Confederations Cup in

Germany and 2012 European Championship in Poland and Ukraine.

Schweinsteiger scored his first international goal in a friendly against Russia on 8 June 2005. He went on to net several crucial goals in major tournaments for Germany. This includes scoring in the 3-1 third place playoff win over Portugal at the 2006 World Cup on home soil. At Euro 2008, he scored goals against Portugal in the quarterfinals and Turkey in the semi-finals. His offensive contributions were recognized at the 2010 World Cup where he tied for the most assists in the tournament with 3, providing for teammates in Germany's run to another third place finish. Two years later at Euro 2012, Schweinsteiger scored Germany's winner against Ukraine in the group stage.

For his performances and achievements at international level, Schweinsteiger was honored with the Silbernes Lorbeerblatt (the highest athletic honor awarded in Germany) in 2006, 2010 and 2014 after winning the World Cup. He was named the German national team Player of the Year in 2010, won the Footballer of the Year award in Germany in 2013, and was voted into the FIFA World Cup Dream Teams in 2010 and the FIFPro World XI teams in 2013 and 2014. Schweinsteiger received other prestigious individual awards like the Bambi Award in 2016 and was inducted into the Bayern Munich Hall of Fame in 2018 after a long and successful club career there.

Bastian Schweinsteiger was a tremendously accomplished and decorated player for the German national team over his 12-year international career from 2004-2016. He was a key figure in Germany's World Cup triumph in 2014 and played big roles in their runs to the semi-finals of the 2006, 2010 and 2012 major tournaments. Scoring crucial goals in high-pressure knockout matches, his scoring record, struggle for the team, and multitude of individual honors cement Schweinsteiger's legacy as one of the greatest German football legends.

Philip Lahm

Philipp Lahm is considered one of the greatest full-backs of all time and a true legend of German football. Born in Munich in 1983, the diminutive defender spent the majority of his professional career with Bayern Munich, the club he joined as a youth player.

Lahm came through the German youth national team ranks, helping the U19 side win the runner-up medal at the 2002 UEFA European U19 Championship. He made his senior international debut for Germany in 2004 at age 20 and was part of the squad for that year's European Championship, though Germany did not advance past the group stage.

It was at the 2006 World Cup, hosted in Germany, where Lahm first made his mark on the big stage. He started all seven matches for the hosts, playing full 90 minutes in each game. He scored the opening goal in the first match against Costa Rica and was named to the Team of the Tournament.

Two years later at Euro 2008, Lahm started every game and scored a dramatic 90th minute winner against Turkey in the semi-finals, though Germany would go on to lose to Spain in the final. He was again named to the Team of the Tournament.

After being named Germany's permanent captain following Michael Ballack's retirement, Lahm led his country to third-place finishes at both the 2010 World Cup and Euro 2012, making the Team of the Tournament both times.

Lahm's crowning achievement came at the 2014 World Cup in Brazil, where he captained Germany to their fourth world title. Though he spent most of the tournament playing as a defensive midfielder under manager Joachim

Low, Lahm returned to his more natural right-back role for the knockout rounds.

Following Germany's 1-0 victory over Argentina in the final, Lahm announced his retirement from international football at the age of just 30, bowing out at the top after earning 113 caps and scoring 5 goals for his country. He later transitioned into an ambassadorial role for Germany's successful bid to host Euro 2024.

At club level with Bayern Munich, Lahm won 8 Bundesliga titles and the 2013 UEFA Champions League as part of an historic treble-winning season under Pep Guardiola. Though naturally a full-back on either flank, his versatility allowed him to play as a defensive midfielder under Guardiola.

Lahm's leadership, consistency, and intelligence on the pitch drew immense praise throughout his career. He formed a prolific partnership with Arjen Robben on Bayern's right flank. His reading of the game, positioning, technical ability and stamina more than made up for his smaller stature.

Many consider Lahm the perfect professional, always putting the team first. He turned down more lucrative offers to remain a one-club man at Bayern out of loyalty. His tireless work ethic and versatility to play almost any position only added to his manager's admiration.

In addition to leading Germany to World Cup glory, Lahm earned a place in the FIFA World Cup All-Star team three times (2006, 2010, 2014). He was voted into the UEFA Team of the Year on five occasions and the FIFPro World XI four times between 2013-2016.

Other major honors include the 2013 FIFA Club World Cup Silver Ball, being named the 2017 German Footballer of the Year, receiving the Silbernes Lorbeerblatt (Germany's highest sporting honor) in 2006, 2010 and 2014, and being voted into the Ballon d'Or Dream Team in 2020. He was also included in IFFHS's World Team of the 2010s Decade.

With his elite reading of the game, technical quality, big-game mentality and unrivaled professionalism both for club and country, Philipp Lahm cemented himself as one of the true legends of German football and arguably the greatest full-back of his generation. His legacy is

The Complete Fan's Companion to EURO 2024

secure as both a World Cup-winning captain and one of Bayern Munich's all-time greats.

Manuel Neuer

Manuel Neuer is widely considered one of the greatest and most influential goalkeepers in the history of the sport. The German shot-stopper has been a trailblazer for the modern sweeper-keeper role, revolutionizing how the position is played with his unique style.

Born in Gelsenkirchen in 1986, Neuer came through the German youth national team ranks. He won the 2009 UEFA European Under-21 Championship, keeping a clean sheet in the 4-0 final victory over England. This led to his senior team debut later that year at age 23.

Neuer was thrust into the starting role at the 2010 World Cup in South Africa after injuries to rivals Rene Adler and Robert Enke. He seized the opportunity, conceding just one goal in the group stage as Germany took a third-place finish. Neuer provided the assist for Miroslav Klose's opening goal in the famous 4-1 win over England.

Two years later at Euro 2012, Neuer played every minute of Germany's run to the semi-finals. He made several crucial saves and set up goals with his long passing and distribution out of the back. Neuer earned a spot on the Team of the Tournament.

It was at the 2014 World Cup in Brazil where Neuer really showcased his sweeper-keeper abilities on the biggest stage. His willingness to race off his line and cut out counterattacks was praised, allowing his teammates to take an aggressive high defensive line. Neuer finished with the Golden Glove award as the tournament's best goalkeeper after Germany won their fourth World Cup title.

In the final against Argentina, Neuer made a number of crucial interventions and clearances outside his box to snuff out Argentinian attacks. He finished the tournament with more completed passes (244) than stars like Lionel Messi and Thomas Muller. Neuer was named to the World Cup All-Star Team and Dream Team.

On the club level, Neuer has been the undisputed starter at Bayern Munich since joining in 2011 from boyhood club Schalke. With Bayern, he has won 10 Bundesliga titles and two Champions League crowns, including the historic 2019/20 treble under Hansi Flick.

Neuer has singled out his work with manager Pep Guardiola as pivotal in transitioning him into the modern sweeper-keeper role. Under Guardiola's guidance, Neuer became increasingly comfortable operating almost as an outfield player and helping to build attacks from the back.

Standing at an imposing 6'4" tall, Neuer has the ideal physical stature and athleticism for a goalkeeper. His reflexes, agility, powerful hands and feet, and shot-stopping abilities are truly elite. Neuer's speed, anticipation, and decision-making allow him to rush off his line and snuff out opposing attacks almost like a sweeper.

When called upon to make more traditional goalkeeper plays, Neuer demonstrates excellent positioning, a commanding leadership presence, and superb skill in one-on-one situations. He is renowned for his penalty-saving abilities and even takes spot-kicks himself in shootouts on occasion.

A former outfield player in his youth, Neuer's technical quality with the ball at his feet is also exemplary. His vision, long distribution, and passing range out of the back enable him to launch counter-attacks or retain possession under pressure.

In addition to his pure shot-stopping and goalkeeping talents, Neuer is praised for his elite mentality, concentration, decision-making, and reading of the game in virtually any scenario. His versatility and ability to adapt his style makes him a true triple-threat keeper.

At age 36, Neuer continues performing at an elite level and shows no signs of slowing down anytime soon. He was voted the IFFHS World's Best Goalkeeper an incredible 7 times between 2013-2020 and was named their Goalkeeper of the Decade for 2011-2020.

Other major individual honors for Neuer include the 2014 World Cup Golden Glove, 5 selections to the UEFA Team of the Year, 4 FIFA FIFPro World XI appearances, and 11 German Goalkeeper of the

Year awards. He was also named the 2011 and 2014 German Footballer of the Year.

In 2020, Neuer was named The Best FIFA Men's Goalkeeper and earned a place on the Ballon d'Or Dream Team. At Euro 2020, he set a tournament record for longest shutout streak at 557 minutes before conceding.

With 117 caps to date for Germany, Neuer is the first German goalkeeper ever to appear at 4 consecutive World Cups from 2010 to 2022. He broke Sepp Maier's national team record for career clean sheets in 2019.

For both his incredible success at club and international level, as well as revolutionizing the sweeper-keeper role, Manuel Neuer has cemented himself as an all-time German football legend. At the peak of his career, many regarded him as simply the best goalkeeper in the world.

Neuer's longevity, game-changing skillset, big tournament performances, and long list of individual and team accolades put him in elite company among the greatest German players ever. He has raised the bar for what is possible from the goalkeeper position in the modern game. It will be lovely to see him play at EURO 2024.

Miroslav Klose

Miroslav Klose is regarded as one of the greatest German football players of all time due to his incredible goalscoring exploits for the national team, especially at World Cup tournaments. The Polish-born striker is the highest scorer in World

Cup finals history with 16 goals across four editions between 2002 and 2014.

Klose finished as the joint-second top scorer at the 2002 World Cup with 5 headed goals, earning him the nickname "Salto-Klose" for his trademark somersault celebrations. This included a hat-trick in Germany's 8-0 thrashing of Saudi Arabia.

Four years later at the 2006 World Cup in Germany, Klose won the Golden Boot as the tournament's top scorer by netting another 5 goals. He scored crucial equalizers against Argentina in the quarterfinals as Germany went on to take third place.

Klose remained prolific at major tournaments for Germany, scoring 4 goals at the 2010 World Cup in South Africa. His strike against England saw him equal Pele for 4th on the all-time World Cup scorers list with 12 goals. Klose then matched Gerd Muller's German record of 14 World Cup goals by netting twice versus Argentina in the quarterfinals.

It was at the 2014 World Cup in Brazil where Klose cemented his legacy as a German legend. Coming off the bench, he scored late equalizers in the group stage to earn draws with Ghana and eventual champions Germany. These two goals saw Klose break Ronaldo's record to become the highest World Cup finals goalscorer of all time with 16 strikes.

Klose scored again in Germany's incredible 7-1 semifinal demolition of hosts Brazil, making him the first player ever to appear in four consecutive World Cup semifinals. He earned a winner's medal as Germany beat Argentina 1-0 after extra time in the final, with Klose substituted off just before the decisive Mario Götze goal.

With 71 goals in 137 appearances for Germany, Klose is comfortably his country's all-time leading scorer, having surpassed the legendary Gerd Muller's tally of 68 goals before the 2014 World Cup. His international goalscoring record included 9 strikes during qualifying for Euro 2012.

While he never won a European Championship, Klose still enjoyed an excellent tournament record on that stage too. He helped Germany to the final of Euro 2008, scoring the winner against Turkey in the semifinals.

Though his club career was far less decorated than his international one, Klose still accomplished a great deal over his 666 games for clubs like Kaiserslautern, Werder Bremen, Bayern Munich and Lazio.

He won two Bundesliga titles with Bayern in 2007/08 and 2009/10, plus the DFB-Pokal Cup in 2007/08. Klose was the leading scorer and Player of the Season in the 2005/06 Bundesliga campaign with 25 goals and 10 assists for Werder Bremen. He finished as the leading assist provider in Germany's top flight on two occasions.

In addition to his goalscoring prowess, Klose stood out for his honesty, sportsmanship and exemplary behavior both on and off the pitch. On multiple occasions, he informed referees when he had illegally scored or gained an advantage, declining penalties or goals he felt had been wrongly awarded.

Klose received several fair play awards from the German FA and other organizations in recognition of his integrity and for setting a positive example, especially for younger players. In 2023, he was presented with the prestigious UEFA President's Award honoring his career achievements.

Beyond his goalscoring records and success at World Cups, Klose's humility, professionalism, and sportsmanlike conduct further enhanced his standing as a true German football legend and role model for the game.

His prime years as an elite striker came in an era that overlapped with other German greats like Michael Ballack, Bastian Schweinsteiger and Philipp Lahm. But Klose carved out his own niche and legacy through his World Cup heroics.

From humble beginnings growing up in Poland before moving to Germany as a teenager, Klose became a prolific striker at the highest level. His aerial prowess, movement, positioning and poacher's instinct in the box made him a nightmare for defenders.

While international competitions were certainly Klose's crowning achievements, he still managed an impressive 256 goals and 134 assists over his 17-year club career in the German, Italian and Saudi leagues.

For his consistent goalscoring, professional conduct and status as the leading World Cup finals marksman in history, Miroslav Klose rightly takes his place among the German national team's all-time legends. His World Cup scoring record may never be matched.

Thomas Müller

Thomas Müller is also considered one of the greatest German footballers of his generation. Born on September 13, 1989 in Weilheim in Oberbayern, West Germany, Müller has spent his entire professional career with Bayern Munich.

Müller has played a variety of attacking roles - as an attacking midfielder, second striker, center forward, and on either wing. He is regarded for his outstanding positioning, teamwork, stamina, and work-rate. Müller has shown remarkable consistency in both scoring and creating goals.

Müller earned his first call-up to the senior German national team in 2010 after progressing through the youth ranks. At the 2010 FIFA World Cup in South Africa, the 21-year-old Müller had a breakthrough tournament. He scored 5 goals in 6 appearances as Germany finished third. Müller won the Golden Boot as the top scorer and the Best Young Player award.

In the 2014 World Cup in Brazil, Müller played a vital role in Germany's title triumph. He scored a hat-trick in the opening 4-0 win over Portugal. Müller ended up with 5 goals, sharing the Silver Boot as the second-highest scorer. He also received the Silver Ball as the second best player and was named to the World Cup All-Star team.

Müller has represented Germany at 4 World Cups - 2010, 2014, 2018 and 2022. His 10 goals at the 2014 and 2010 tournaments made him only the third player to score at least 5 goals in each of his first two World Cups, after Teófilo Cubillas and teammate Miroslav Klose.

At the European Championships, Müller featured in the 2012, 2016, and 2020 editions for Germany. Though he didn't score at Euro 2016, he had 9 goals in the qualifying campaign as Germany topped their group.

Müller has earned 128 caps for Germany since his debut in 2010, scoring 45 goals which ranks him 8th on the all-time German scoring list. He was a key member of the 2014 World Cup winning side, regarded as one of the greatest German teams ever.

Müller's playing style is truly unique. He lacks elite physical attributes but makes up for it with his tactical intelligence, positioning, movement, composure and consistency in scoring and creating goals. He describes his role as a "Raumdeuter" or space interpreter - finding gaps in opposition defenses to exploit.

Former managers have praised Müller's tremendous mental strength, tactical awareness and ability to remain impervious to pressure. Though not particularly skilled at dribbling, his intelligent runs and clinical finishing have made him a prolific scorer at the highest level.

In addition to his scoring prowess, Müller has been lauded for his defensive work-rate, stamina and overall team play. His constant communication on the pitch earned him the nickname "Radio Müller" from an assistant coach.

At club level, Müller has been a one-club man starting his career with Bayern's youth academy in 2000. He made his first-team debut in 2008 and has since won a staggering 33 trophies with the German giants - the most by any German player.

Müller has won 11 Bundesliga titles, 6 DFB-Pokals, 6 DFL-Supercups, 2 UEFA Champions Leagues, 1 UEFA Super Cup and 1 FIFA Club World Cup with Bayern Munich. His tallies for goals and assists put him among the club's all-time leaders.

Some of Müller's individual accolades include the 2010 Golden Boot and Best Young Player at the World Cup, Golden Boot at the 2010 DFB-Pokal, 2020 UEFA Super Cup Man of the Match, 2021-22 Bayern Munich Player of the Season and being named to the UEFA Champions League and Bundesliga Teams of the Season multiple times.

At 34 years old, Müller remains a key part of the Bayern Munich and German national team set-ups. He was recalled to the national team in 2021 after a two-year absence and featured at the pandemic-delayed Euro 2020 as well as the 2022 World Cup in Qatar.

With his goal-scoring prowess, versatility, tactical awareness and winning mentality, Thomas Müller has cemented his legacy as an all-time German football great. His unconventional style, success at the highest levels, and record-breaking achievements make him one of the most decorated and impactful players of his era.

The Complete Fan's Companion to EURO 2024

Chapter 10: German Football Culture

German football has a rich and distinctive culture that has played a major role in the nation's sustained success on the international stage. From the grassroots level up through the professional ranks, there are several unique aspects that make the German football system stand out.

One of the defining pillars is the emphasis on youth development across the country. The creation of elite youth academies at top clubs like Bayern Munich, Borussia Dortmund, and Schalke has allowed for the identification and nurturing of talented youngsters from an early age. However, this focus starts even before the academies, with a massive participatory base.

Germany has over 25,000 football clubs involving nearly 2 million active youth players between the ages of 7-19. Children take up the sport from a very young age, playing organized matches by age 5 or 6 in some areas. There is an incredible density of clubs, even in small towns and villages across the nation. This allows virtually every child the opportunity to play, honing their skills in a community environment from the start.

The coaching and training of these young players follows a remarkably systematic and innovative approach. The German Football Association oversees coaching education to implement a uniform national philosophy emphasizing technical ability, tactics, decision-making and mental development. Creative expression on the ball is encouraged from an early age, backed by sports science. Teams prioritize possession-based attacking football over rigid defensive tactics.

As players progress through the youth ranks, the most talented are filtered into professional academies. Top clubs invest heavily into state-of-the-art facilities and scouting networks to identify the best prospects across Germany. The academies provide an immersive training environment with a heavy focus on sports science, data analysis, nutrition and psychological development complementing the on-pitch work.

What is unique is the structure allowing close integration between the academies and first teams. Young talents get opportunities to train alongside senior stars, easing their transition. The Bundesliga also has specific rules mandating the inclusion of homegrown under-23 players in each matchday squad. This incentivizes clubs to blood youngsters on the big stage.

The academies, combined with excellent coaching implementation of the national philosophy from grassroots up, have produced highly effective mechanisms for identifying and developing generational talents like Toni Kroos, Thomas Müller, Manuel Neuer and many others who have guided Germany's success.

Transitioning to the professional level, the cultural environment within the structure of the Bundesliga and its clubs has also cultivated success. The 50+1 ownership rule prevents majority corporate or foreign ownership of clubs. This ensures fanbases retain control, with established members comprising the voting board. Clubs view themselves as community representatives with a cultural identity, rather than just commercial franchises.

On the business side, strict financial sustainability regulations and even distribution of TV revenues have prevented a runaway hierarchy forming. This allows challengers like Dortmund, Leipzig or Monchengladbach to push traditional giants like Bayern Munich more than some one-team dominated leagues. The competitiveness retains interest and player motivation across the league. Take a look at Bayer Leverkusen who just won the Bundesliga.

The terraced stadium designs also create an intense atmosphere conducive to high-paced, attack-minded football. Most grounds have standing areas and low ticket prices making for impassioned, volatile home supports motivating energetic performances. Coaches instill mentally tough, high-pressing styles to harness that motivation.

The intense pressing, counter-pressing and hard running has become the modern German hallmark, employed by the biggest club and national sides under coaches like Jurgen Klopp and Thomas Tuchel. Yet it is combined with tactical discipline, efficiency in transitions and set-pieces, and a knack for decisive "Germani" efficiency in attack cultivated from the grassroots upwards.

At international level, the impact of Germany's deep-rooted football culture culminates in *Die Mannschaft*'s ability to consistently regenerate world-class squads through each cycle. Their youth development systems always have a fresh production line of immensely talented players developed in the unique German footballing environment from boyhood. This makes manager transitions smooth and sustained success achievable.

Combined with operational excellence across areas like sports science, psychological profiling, data-driven analysis and meticulous preparation, Germany are able to continually produce hard-working, technically gifted, mentally tough teams ready to implement strategic game-plans to maximum effect on the grandest stages. Their mentality was encapsulated by the 7-1 demolition of Brazil in 2014 - a seismic result displaying all the elements cultivated from Germany's deeply-embedded football culture.

The Complete Fan's Companion to EURO 2024

Chapter 11: Future Host Nations

In October 2023, UEFA announced the host nations for the upcoming editions of the tournament, Euro 2028 and Euro 2032. These decisions were made after a thorough bidding process and careful consideration by the UEFA Executive Committee.

Euro 2028: United Kingdom and Republic of Ireland

After an unopposed joint bid, the United Kingdom (England, Northern Ireland, Scotland, and Wales) and the Republic of Ireland were unanimously selected to host the 2028 UEFA European Championship. This will be the third time England plays host to the event, following Euro 1996 and matches during Euro 2020 (including the final). It will also be the second time fixtures will be played in Scotland, where four ties in the 2020 competition took place. Notably, games will be held in Northern Ireland, the Republic of Ireland, and Wales for the first time.

The bid process for Euro 2028 initially saw three proposals from England, Northern Ireland, the Republic of Ireland, Scotland, and Wales (joint bid), Turkey, and Russia. However, Turkey withdrew its submission to focus on a joint bid with Italy for Euro 2032, and Russia's bid was deemed ineligible due to the ongoing UEFA ban on Russian teams and the national team following the country's invasion of Ukraine.

Venues:

The Complete Fan's Companion to EURO 2024

The Euro 2028 tournament will be played across ten stadiums in nine host cities. The venues selected are:

1. Wembley Stadium (London, England) - Capacity: 90,652
2. Tottenham Hotspur Stadium (London, England) - Capacity: 62,322
3. Millennium Stadium (Cardiff, Wales) - Capacity: 73,952
4. City of Manchester Stadium (Manchester, England) - Capacity: 61,000
5. Everton Stadium (Liverpool, England) - New stadium, Capacity: 52,888
6. St James' Park (Newcastle, England) - Capacity: 52,305
7. Villa Park (Birmingham, England) - To be renovated, Capacity: 52,190

8. Hampden Park (Glasgow, Scotland) - Capacity: 52,032

9. Aviva Stadium (Dublin, Republic of Ireland) - Capacity: 51,711

10. Casement Park (Belfast, Northern Ireland) - To be renovated, Capacity: 30,000

The vision for Euro 2028 is "Football for all. Football for good. Football for the future." The five host associations aim to increase participation, engagement, and revenue across the game, leaving a lasting legacy beyond 2028. Through the "Football for all" policy, they plan to grow a more inclusive game with new and upgraded facilities, increased numbers of referees and coaches, and more opportunities for grassroots players, particularly those with disabilities.

The "Football for good" initiative will focus on delivering tangible long-term benefits for society, inspiring sustainable, thriving football clubs and communities. During the tournament, a compact and connected travel plan will ensure 80% of supporters can attend matches via public transport, with a match schedule designed to reduce emissions.

The "Football for the future" aspect focuses on economic benefits, aiming to generate €3 billion across the ten host cities and beyond, creating education, training, and sustainability initiatives with government support.

Euro 2032: Italy and Turkey

After being the sole bidders, Italy and Turkey were appointed as joint hosts for the 2032 UEFA European Championship. This will be the fourth time that European Championship matches are played in Italy, who previously hosted the 1968 and 1980 tournaments, as well as matches during Euro 2020 in Rome. For Turkey, it will be the first time hosting the prestigious competition.

The bid process for Euro 2032 initially saw three bids from Italy, Turkey, and Russia, but Russia's bid was deemed ineligible due to the ongoing UEFA ban.

The bidders have proposed 20 stadiums, of which 10 will be chosen to stage matches, five per country, by October 2026. The proposed venues are:

The Complete Fan's Companion to EURO 2024

Italy:

1. Milan: Stadio San Siro - Giuseppe Meazza

2. Rome: Stadio Olimpico

3. Bari: Stadio San Nicola (to be renovated)

4. Naples: Stadio Diego Armando Maradona (to be renovated)

5. Florence: Stadio Artemio Franchi (new stadium)

6. Turin: Juventus Stadium

7. Genoa: Stadio Luigi Ferraris (to be renovated)

8. Verona: Stadio Marcantonio Bentegodi (to be renovated)

9. Bologna: Stadio Renato Dall'Ara (new stadium)

10. Cagliari: Stadio Sant'Elia (new stadium)

Turkey:

1. Istanbul: Atatürk Olympic Stadium (to be renovated)

2. Ankara: New Ankara Stadium (new stadium)

3. Istanbul: Ali Sami Yen Stadium

4. Istanbul: Sükrü Saraçoglu Stadium

5. Bursa: Timsah Arena

6. Trabzon: Şenol Güneş Sport Complex

7. Konya: Konya Metropolitan Stadium

8. Gaziantep: Gaziantep Kalyon Stadium

9. Eskişehir: Eskişehir Stadium

10. Antalya: Antalya Stadium

Under the motto "Play as One," the Italian Football Federation (FIGC) and the Turkish Football Federation (TFF) aim to offer the ultimate Euro experience to fans, establishing new bridges of friendship and leaving a lasting contribution to the football legacy.

Both associations will focus on grassroots development programs, aiming to ensure growth at the lower levels of the football pyramid while creating opportunities for their most talented young players to reach their potential.

The tournament will be used to reach more children through development camps and centers, promoting inclusion and a clear pathway into the game for disadvantaged young people, while also offering social support and increasing links between schools and amateur clubs.

For Euro 2028, it is unclear which host teams may qualify automatically. One plan being considered is that all five host teams (England, Northern Ireland, Republic of Ireland, Scotland, and Wales) may enter qualifying, with two automatic spots held in reserve for hosts which fail to qualify. Should three or more host teams fail to qualify, the spots would be awarded to the best-performing hosts.

The Complete Fan's Companion to EURO 2024

As co-hosts for Euro 2032, Italy and Turkey have qualified automatically, while the remaining spots will be determined by a qualifying tournament.

The UEFA European Championship continues to be a prestigious and highly anticipated event, with the 2028 and 2032 editions set to be hosted by the United Kingdom, Republic of Ireland, Italy, and Turkey. These host nations have outlined ambitious plans to leave a lasting legacy, promote inclusivity, and further develop the game at all levels, ensuring the Euros remain a celebration of football for years to come.

The Complete Fan's Companion to EURO 2024

Chapter 12: Euro 2024 Match Officials

The referees who will officiate matches at the Euro 2024 tournament have not yet been assigned specific games. The list of referees includes Jesús Gil Manzano from Spain, Marco Guida from Italy, István Kovács from Romania, Ivan Kružliak from Slovakia, François Letexier from France, Danny Makkelie from the Netherlands, Szymon Marciniak from Poland, Halil Umut Meler from Turkey, Glenn Nyberg from Sweden, Michael Oliver from England, Daniele Orsato from Italy, Sandro Schärer from Switzerland, Daniel Siebert from Germany, Artur Soares Dias from Portugal, Anthony Taylor from England, Facundo Tello from Argentina, Clément Turpin from France, and Slavko Vinčić from

Slovenia. Felix Zwayer is another referee from Germany who will work the Euro 2024 matches. As this book is being written, these referees have not been told which specific games they will oversee during the tournament.

The Complete Fan's Companion to EURO 2024

Chapter 13: The Euro 2024 Match Symbols

The official Euro 2024 mascot is a teddy bear wearing shorts named "Albärt". The name "Albärt" was chosen after a public vote was done. It beat out other name options like "Bärnheart" "Bärnardo", and "Herzi von Bär".

For the tournament's official match ball, Adidas and UEFA revealed the "Fussballliebe" ball on November 15, 2023. The German name "Fussballliebe" translates to "Love of football". The ball has a black design with red, orange blue and green curved shapes meant to represent the vibrancy of the nations qualified for Euro 2024 and the love fans have for the sport. It is made from sustainable organic materials. The ball has sensors inside which can track the ball's movement to assist match officials with decisions.

Conclusion

Euro 2024 promises to be a thrilling and memorable tournament hosted by Germany. After years of preparation, the stage is set for Europe's top national teams to battle it out to be crowned champions.

The host nation Germany will be among the favorites, fielding a talented squad determined to win their first European title since 1996 on home soil. However, they will face stiff competition from the likes of reigning champions Italy, World Cup winners France, England's golden generation, and other traditional powerhouses like Spain, Portugal and the Netherlands.

Emerging forces such as Belgium, Croatia and Denmark have also shown they can compete with the elite on the biggest stages. And there's always the potential for a dark horse nation to capture the hearts of neutrals with an inspirational run to the latter stages.

Whichever teams make it to the final in Berlin, fans can expect top quality action, drama, and brilliant individual performances that will live long in the memory. The state-of-the-art stadiums across Germany will provide the perfect setting for the best in European football to entertain a truly global audience.

When the final whistle blows, not only will one nation get to call themselves European champions, but the tournament as a whole will hopefully inspire the next generation of players and leave a lasting legacy by enhancing Germany's infrastructure and passion for the

The Complete Fan's Companion to EURO 2024

game. Euro 2024 has all the ingredients to be an unforgettable spectacle for the beautiful game.

See you in Germany. Danke!

The Complete Fan's Companion to EURO 2024

REVIEW

Dear Reader,

We really appreciate you purchasing our book and taking the time to read it. Now that you've finished, we kindly request that you leave an honest review. Positive feedback is incredibly helpful, but we genuinely value all constructive opinions.

Your review plays a crucial role in shaping our future writing efforts. It provides invaluable insights into what resonates with readers like yourself. Moreover, it aids fellow book lovers in making informed decisions about their next read. A thoughtful review can introduce our work to a wider audience.

The Complete Fan's Companion to EURO 2024

Each review contributes to building a community of engaged readers who share perspectives and connect over the shared joy of literature. Your words hold the power to inspire others and serve as a guide, celebrating the beauty of open dialogue and heartfelt expression.

We appreciate you being part of this journey. Your voice matters immensely to us and to countless other readers searching for their next great find.

Printed in Great Britain
by Amazon